The Golf Mindset
Mastering Mental Toughness
on the Course

ISBN: 979-8-89034-766-4

Legal & Disclaimer

Table of Contents

Introduction

The Importance of Mental Toughness in Golf

Golf is one of the most mentally challenging sports in the world. It requires players to have a unique combination of physical skill, mental fortitude, and emotional control. While many golfers spend countless hours perfecting their swing and improving their physical ability, very few invest the same amount of time in developing their mental game.

Golf is a game that demands mental strength and focus. Whether you are an amateur or a professional golfer, the ability to stay mentally tough and focused on the course is crucial to playing good golf. In fact, many golfers have found that the difference between winning and losing often comes down to mental toughness. In this book, we will focus on mastering the mental game of golf.

Why Mental Strategies are Important for Experienced Golfers

The mental aspect of golf is often overlooked, but it is just as important as the physical aspect. In fact, many professional golfers credit their success to their mental game. The ability to stay focused, manage emotions, and make smart decisions under pressure can mean the difference between winning and losing.

Experienced golfers face unique mental challenges on the course. They have likely faced defeat and disappointment before and may struggle with self-doubt or negative self-talk. Additionally, as golfers get older, they may experience changes in physical abilities that can impact their mental game. Mental strategies can help experienced golfers overcome these challenges and improve their performance.

Developing mental toughness is not something that happens overnight. It requires consistent effort and practice, just like any other skill. However, the benefits of mental toughness are manifold, and they can make a huge difference in your golf performance.

One of the most important aspects of mental toughness is developing laser focus. When you are playing golf, you need to be fully present in the moment and focused on the shot at hand. This means being able to block out distractions and stay focused on the task at hand.

Visualization is another key component of mental toughness. By visualizing the shot before you take it, you can create a mental picture of what you want to achieve. This not only helps you stay focused, but it also helps you to execute the shot more effectively.

Positive thinking is also crucial to mental toughness. By maintaining a positive mindset, you can overcome obstacles and stay motivated even in difficult situations. This is especially important in golf, where a single bad shot can easily snowball into a string of bad shots. We will explore the importance of having a positive attitude and developing a growth mindset. We will also discuss how to overcome self-doubt and negative self-talk, and how to stay focused and present on the course.

In addition to these mental exercises, it is also important to develop mental stamina. Golf can be a physically and mentally challenging game, and you need to have the mental endurance to stay focused and sharp throughout the round. This requires training and practice just like physical stamina.

The Role of Mental Preparation in Golf

Golf is a game of precision and strategy. It requires a high level of mental toughness and focus to be successful. Mental preparation plays a crucial role in a golfer's game, as it helps to build confidence and prepare the mind for the challenges that lie ahead.

Mental preparation can help players to:

Stay focused on the task at hand

Manage their emotions and avoid getting distracted by negative thoughts

Make better decisions on the course

Stay motivated and confident, even when things are not going well

Relaxation techniques can also be helpful in maintaining mental toughness on the golf course. By learning to stay calm and relaxed under pressure, you can avoid getting too caught up in your emotions and stay focused on the task at hand.

Ultimately, developing a strong and resilient golf mindset is essential to success on the course. Mastering the mental game of golf is just as important as developing physical skills. By overcoming mental obstacles and building confidence through mental exercises, you can improve your golf performance and achieve your goals. Whether you are a beginner or a seasoned pro, the mental game of golf is critical to your success, and developing mental toughness is key to mastering it. Experienced golfers face unique mental challenges that can impact their performance on the course. This book provides practical strategies for improving your mental game and taking your golf game to the next level.

The Purpose of the Book

The Golf Mindset: Mastering Mental Toughness on the Course is a book designed for golfers who want to strengthen their minds and optimize their golf performance using mental game techniques. This book is a culmination of years of research, experience, and expertise from the most successful golfers and coaches. It is a comprehensive guide on how to develop laser focus, visualization skills, positive thinking, mental stamina, relaxation techniques, and mental toughness to help golfers achieve their full potential on the course.

The purpose of this book is to provide golfers with the tools and strategies needed to develop a strong and resilient golf mindset. The book aims to help golfers overcome mental obstacles on the course, build confidence, mindfulness, and achieve their goals by training their minds. The book is divided into chapters that cover different aspects of the mental game of golf, including visualization, positive thinking, mental stamina, relaxation techniques, and mindfulness meditation.

Chapter one focuses on developing laser focus, which is crucial for golfers when playing the game. This chapter outlines the importance of concentration, attention, and focus on the course and provides practical exercises to help golfers improve their focus.

Chapter two discusses visualization techniques for improved focus. Visualization is an essential mental skill that helps golfers see themselves making perfect shots and performing at their best. This chapter provides several visualization exercises to help golfers improve their visualization skills.

Chapter three highlights the power of positive thinking in golf. Positive thinking is a vital mental skill that helps golfers stay optimistic, confident, and focused, even under pressure. This chapter provides several strategies for developing a positive attitude, overcoming negative self-talk, and building self-confidence.

Chapter four introduces mental stamina training for golfers. Golf is not just a physical sport but also a mental game. The ability to concentrate, focus, and maintain energy throughout the game is essential for golfers to succeed in the sport. Therefore, mental stamina training is crucial for golfers who aim to improve their game and overcome challenges such as long tournaments, high-pressure situations, and unexpected setbacks Mental stamina is the ability to maintain focus, concentration, and energy throughout the game, especially during long tournaments.

. This chapter introduces mental stamina training for golfers and provides several exercises that can help them develop endurance and resilience.

Chapter five discusses relaxation techniques for better golf performance. Relaxation is important for golfers as it helps reduce anxiety, tension, and stress, which can affect their performance. This chapter provides several relaxation exercises, including deep breathing, progressive muscle relaxation, and visualization.

Chapter six focuses on developing a strong and resilient golf mindset. A strong mindset is essential for golfers as it helps them stay motivated, focused, and confident, even when facing challenges or setbacks. This chapter provides several mental exercises and strategies to help golfers develop a strong and resilient mindset.

Chapter seven focuses on overcoming mental obstacles on the golf course. Mental obstacles, such as fear, anxiety, and self-doubt, can affect a golfer's performance. This chapter provides several strategies for overcoming mental obstacles and building mental toughness.

Chapter eight discusses building confidence through mental exercises in golf. Confidence is essential for golfers as it helps them perform at their best and achieve their goals. This chapter provides several confidence-building exercises, including self-talk, visualization, and goal-setting.

Chapter nine introduces mindfulness and meditation for golfers. Mindfulness and meditation are powerful mental skills that help golfers stay focused, calm, and present on the course. This chapter provides several mindfulness exercises and meditation techniques to help golfers develop these skills.

Chapter ten focuses on goal setting and achievement in golf through mindset training. Goal setting is essential for golfers as it helps them stay motivated, focused, and committed to their goals. This chapter provides several strategies for setting and achieving goals using mindset training.

Finally, chapter eleven discusses the mental game of golf and strategies for success. This chapter brings together all the mental skills and strategies covered in the book and provides a comprehensive framework for developing a strong and resilient golf mindset.

The Golf Mindset: Mastering Mental Toughness on the Course is a comprehensive guide that provides golfers with the tools and strategies needed to develop a strong and resilient golf mindset. Whether you're a beginner or a seasoned pro, this book can help you improve your mental game and achieve your full potential on the course.

The Target Audience

As a golfer, you know that the sport is not just about physical strength and ability. Golf requires a strong mindset that can endure the challenges and pressures of the game. This is why we have created this book, The Golf Mindset: Mastering Mental Toughness on the Course, to help golfers strengthen their minds and optimize their golf performance with mental game.

Our target audience is golfers who want to develop laser focus, visualization, positive thinking, mental stamina, relaxation, and mental toughness with mental exercises. We understand that golfers come from different backgrounds, ages, and skill levels. However, our book is designed to cater to all golfers who want to improve their mental game and take their golf skills to the next level.

Our book covers a wide range of niches that are crucial for golfers who want to master their mental toughness on the course. We provide golf visualization techniques that can help improve focus and concentration during the game. We also discuss the power of positive thinking in golf, which can help golfers maintain a positive attitude and overcome any obstacles during the game.

Mental stamina is another essential aspect of golf that we address in our book. We provide mental stamina training for golfers to help them stay focused and mentally alert throughout the game. Additionally, we offer relaxation techniques for better golf performance, which can help golfers stay relaxed and calm under pressure.

Developing a strong and resilient golf mindset is a vital part of our book, as we believe that mental toughness is the key to success in golf. We offer strategies for overcoming mental obstacles on the golf course, building confidence through mental exercises, and mindfulness and meditation for golfers.

Our book also covers goal setting and achievement in golf through mindset training, as we believe that setting goals is an effective way to improve your golf performance. Finally, we provide strategies for success in the mental game of golf that can help golfers optimize their golf performance and achieve their full potential.

In conclusion, our book, The Golf Mindset: Mastering Mental Toughness on the Course, is designed to provide golfers with the necessary tools and techniques to strengthen their minds and optimize their golf performance with mental game. Whether you are a beginner or an experienced golfer, our book has something for everyone who wants to improve their golf game by mastering their mental toughness on the course.

Chapter 1

The Fundamentals of Golf Mindset

Understanding the Mind-Body Connection

As a golfer, you know that the sport requires both physical and mental prowess. But did you know that the mind and body are interconnected, and that mastering the connection between the two can significantly improve your golf game?

The mind-body connection refers to the relationship between your thoughts, emotions, and physical body. In golf, this connection is essential because the way you think and feel can affect the way you swing, putt, and ultimately, perform on the course.

Developing a strong mind-body connection requires focus, visualization, positive thinking, and mental stamina. By practicing mental exercises and relaxation techniques, you can train your mind to stay calm, focused, and mentally tough on the golf course.

One of the most effective ways to strengthen the mind-body connection is through visualization. Visualization is a technique that involves creating mental images of yourself successfully executing a shot or achieving a goal. By visualizing yourself hitting the perfect shot over and over again, you can train your brain to believe that it is possible, which can improve your confidence and focus on the course.

Positive thinking is another critical component of the mind-body connection in golf. By focusing on positive thoughts and outcomes, you can shift your mindset from one of doubt and fear to one of confidence and optimism. This can help you stay calm and focused, even in high-pressure situations.

Mental stamina is also crucial for golfers. The mental game of golf requires you to stay focused and mentally strong for an extended period, which can be challenging. By practicing mental exercises and mindfulness techniques, you can improve your ability to stay focused and relaxed, even during stressful situations.

Overcoming mental obstacles on the golf course is another important part of the mind-body connection. Whether it's a bad shot or a missed putt, golfers must learn to let go of negative thoughts and emotions and move forward. By practicing mindfulness and meditation, you can develop the mental resilience needed to overcome obstacles and stay focused on your goals.

The mind-body connection is a crucial component of golf performance. By mastering this connection through visualization, positive thinking, mental stamina training, relaxation techniques, and mental exercises, you can develop a strong and resilient golf mindset that will help you achieve your goals on the course.

Developing a Positive Attitude

A positive attitude is one of the most important components of a successful golfer's mental game. It can help you stay focused and motivated, even in the face of challenging shots or difficult weather conditions. By developing a positive attitude, you can optimize your performance on the golf course and achieve your goals.

One of the first steps in developing a positive attitude is to focus on the present moment. This means letting go of any negative thoughts or distractions that may be holding you back. Instead, try to stay focused on the shot at hand, visualizing the ball landing exactly where you want it to go.

Visualization is another powerful tool for developing a positive attitude. By imagining yourself hitting the perfect shot, you can build confidence and overcome any doubts or fears that may be holding you back. This can be done through mental exercises, such as visualization techniques or guided imagery, which can help you improve your focus and concentration.

Mental stamina is also important for developing a positive attitude. This involves training your mind to stay focused and alert, even during long rounds or challenging conditions. This can be achieved through relaxation techniques, such as deep breathing or mindfulness exercises, which can help you stay calm and centered no matter what happens on the course.

Building a strong and resilient golf mindset also requires overcoming mental obstacles, such as self-doubt, fear, or frustration. This can be done through goal setting and achievement, which can help you stay motivated and focused on your goals. By setting realistic goals and tracking your progress, you can build confidence and overcome any mental barriers that may be holding you back.

Finally, mindfulness and meditation can be powerful tools for developing a positive attitude. By practicing mindfulness, you can learn to stay present and focused, even during stressful situations. This can help you stay relaxed and mentally tough, even when faced with challenging shots or difficult conditions.

In conclusion, developing a positive attitude is essential for optimizing your golf performance and achieving your goals. By focusing on the present moment, visualizing success, building mental stamina, overcoming obstacles, and practicing mindfulness and meditation, you can develop a strong and resilient golf mindset that will help you succeed on and off the course.

Setting Realistic Goals

Setting goals is an essential part of achieving success in any venture, and golf is no exception. However, it is crucial to set realistic goals that align with your skill level and abilities. Unrealistic goals can lead to frustration, disappointment, and loss of motivation. In this subchapter, we will discuss how to set realistic goals that will help you improve your golf game and achieve success on the course.

Assess Your Current Skill Level

The first step in setting realistic goals is to assess your current skill level. Be honest with yourself about your strengths and weaknesses in golf. Analyze your swing, your short game, your putting, and your mental game. Identify areas that need improvement and areas where you excel.

Set Specific and Measurable Goals

Once you have assessed your current skill level, set specific and measurable goals that align with your abilities. For example, instead of setting a goal to shoot under par, set a goal to improve your score by one stroke per round. This goal is specific, measurable, and achievable.

Break Down Your Goals

Breaking down your goals into smaller, more manageable tasks can help you stay motivated and focused. For example, if your goal is to improve your putting, break it down into smaller tasks such as practicing your putting for 30 minutes a day, or focusing on your alignment and stroke.

Track Your Progress

Tracking your progress is essential to achieving your goals. Keep a record of your scores, your practice sessions, and the areas you are improving. This will help you stay motivated and focused on your goals.

Adjust Your Goals as Needed

It is essential to adjust your goals as needed. If you are consistently achieving your goals, consider setting more challenging goals. If you are struggling to achieve your goals, reassess your current skill level and adjust your goals accordingly.

Conclusion

Setting realistic goals is crucial to achieving success in golf. Assess your current skill level, set specific and measurable goals, break down your goals into smaller tasks, track your progress, and adjust your goals as needed. With a strong and resilient golf mindset and realistic goals, you can achieve success on the course.

The Power of Visualization

Visualization is one of the most powerful tools a golfer can use to improve their performance on the course. The ability to see shots in your mind's eye before you hit them can help you to develop laser focus and improve your golf game. Visualizing shots can help to build confidence and reduce anxiety, allowing you to perform at your best under pressure.

To begin practicing visualization, start by closing your eyes and imagining yourself standing on the first tee. See the fairway stretching out in front of you, the trees lining the course, and the flag waving in the distance. Take a deep breath and visualize your perfect shot. See the ball soaring through the air, landing softly on the fairway, and rolling towards the green. Imagine the sound of the ball hitting the clubface and the feel of a perfect strike.

As you continue to practice visualization, try to incorporate all of your senses. See the colors of the course, feel the wind on your face, and hear the sounds of the birds chirping in the trees. By engaging all of your senses, you can create a more vivid and realistic picture in your mind, which can help to improve your focus and concentration.

Visualization can also be used to improve your putting. Imagine standing over a putt, seeing the line and speed of the ball, and feeling the putter in your hands. Visualize the ball rolling towards the hole and dropping in for a birdie. By practicing this visualization technique regularly, you can build confidence and improve your putting performance.

Positive thinking is also an important component of visualization. By focusing on positive outcomes and seeing yourself succeeding, you can build confidence and reduce anxiety. When you visualize shots, imagine them going exactly as you want them to. Focus on the positive aspects of your game and visualize yourself succeeding on each shot.

In conclusion, visualization is a powerful tool for golfers who want to improve their mental game and optimize their performance on the course. By practicing visualization regularly, golfers can develop laser focus, build confidence, reduce anxiety, and improve their overall golf game. Incorporate visualization into your mental game routine and watch your performance on the course soar.

The Role of Mental Toughness

Mental toughness is essential for golfers who want to optimize their performance on the golf course. It involves developing the ability to remain focused, positive, and relaxed even in the face of challenges and setbacks. Mental toughness helps you stay in the present moment, avoid distractions, and maintain your confidence and composure throughout your game.

Developing mental toughness requires consistent practice and training. Here are some mental exercises that can help you strengthen your mind and build your mental toughness:

1. Visualization: Visualization techniques involve mentally rehearsing your shots before you take them. This helps you develop laser focus and stay in the present moment. Visualize yourself hitting the perfect shot, and then execute it.

2. Positive Thinking: The power of positive thinking cannot be overstated. Focus on your strengths and your successes, and use positive self-talk to boost your confidence and motivation.

3. Mental Stamina Training: Mental stamina is the ability to maintain your focus and energy over the course of a long game. Practice staying mentally alert and engaged throughout your game, even when you're feeling tired or frustrated.

4. Relaxation Techniques: Relaxation exercises such as deep breathing, progressive muscle relaxation, and meditation can help you stay calm and focused under pressure.

5. Overcoming Mental Obstacles: Golfers often face mental obstacles such as fear, doubt, and anxiety. Developing a strong and resilient mindset can help you overcome these obstacles and maintain your confidence and composure.

6. Goal Setting and Achievement: Setting clear goals and developing a plan to achieve them is an essential part of mental toughness training. Focus on your strengths and your areas for improvement, and develop a plan to achieve your goals.

7. Mindfulness and Meditation: Mindfulness and meditation practices can help you stay present and focused, even in the midst of distractions and challenges.

By practicing these mental exercises and developing a strong and resilient mindset, you can optimize your golf performance and achieve your goals on the course. Remember, mental toughness is not something you're born with - it's something you can develop and strengthen with consistent practice and training.

Developing Laser Focus

The Importance of Focus in Golf

One of the key elements to achieving success in golf is focus. Focus is the ability to concentrate on the task at hand, without being distracted by external factors. In golf, focus is critical because it allows you to stay in the present moment and make the most of every shot.

Developing Laser Focus

To develop laser focus, golfers need to practice mental exercises that help them stay in the zone. Visualization techniques are a great way to improve focus, as they allow you to create mental images of the shot you want to make. Positive thinking is also important, as it helps you stay confident and focused on your goals.

Mental Stamina Needed

Golf is a mentally demanding sport, and building mental stamina is essential to achieving success. Mental stamina is the ability to maintain focus and concentration over a prolonged period of time. Golfers can build mental stamina by practicing relaxation techniques, such as deep breathing and meditation.

Stay Relaxed and Mentally Tough

To stay relaxed and mentally tough on the golf course, golfers need to develop a strong and resilient mindset. This involves overcoming mental obstacles, building confidence through mental exercises, and setting goals for achievement. Mindfulness and meditation are also effective techniques for staying mentally tough and focused during a round of golf.

The Power of Positive Thinking

Positive thinking is a powerful tool for golfers, as it helps them stay confident and focused on their goals. Golfers who practice positive thinking are more likely to achieve success on the course, as they are better able to maintain a positive attitude, even in the face of adversity.

Relaxation Techniques for Better Golf Performance

Relaxation techniques, such as deep breathing and meditation, are effective ways to improve golf performance. When you are relaxed, you are better able to stay focused and concentrate on your shots. Golfers who practice relaxation techniques are also less likely to become distracted by external factors, which can negatively impact their performance.

In conclusion, focus is a critical component of golf performance. To achieve success on the course, golfers need to develop laser focus, mental stamina, and a strong and resilient mindset. By practicing relaxation techniques, visualization, positive thinking, and mindfulness, golfers can optimize their mental game and achieve their goals on the course.

Techniques for Improving Focus

The ability to maintain focus is essential in golf. You need to stay focused throughout the entire game, from the first tee shot to the final putt. However, focusing on the game for an extended period can be challenging, especially when external factors distract you. Therefore, as a golfer, you need to develop techniques to improve your focus.

Develop Laser Focus

Laser focus is the ability to concentrate entirely on one task while ignoring distractions. To develop laser focus, you need to train your mind to stay on task, and avoid getting sidetracked. You can do this by practicing mindfulness, which involves focusing on the present moment.

Visualization

Visualization is a technique that involves creating a mental image of the outcome you want to achieve. By visualizing the shot you want to make, you help your mind and body work together to achieve it. Visualization helps you to improve your focus by focusing your mind on the task at hand.

Positive Thinking

Positive thinking involves focusing on the positive outcomes of a situation. When you focus on positive outcomes, it helps you to stay motivated and focused on your goals. Positive thinking can help you to maintain your focus during the game, and it can also help you to overcome mental obstacles.

Mental Stamina Training

Mental stamina training involves practicing mental exercises that help you to build endurance and resilience in your mind. Mental stamina training can help you to maintain your focus throughout the game, even when fatigue sets in.

Relaxation Techniques

Relaxation techniques can help you to stay relaxed and focused during the game. By practicing relaxation techniques, you can reduce stress and anxiety, which can distract you from the game.

Overcoming Mental Obstacles

Mental obstacles can distract you from the game and affect your performance. To overcome these obstacles, you need to develop a strong and resilient mindset. You can do this by practicing mental exercises that help you to stay focused and motivated.

Goal Setting

Setting goals is essential in golf. By setting goals, you give yourself something to work towards, which can help you to stay focused and motivated. Goal setting also helps you to measure your progress and identify areas that need improvement.

In conclusion, improving your focus is essential in golf. By practicing mental exercises and techniques, you can develop a strong and resilient mindset that will help you to stay focused and motivated throughout the game. With a focused and resilient mindset, you can overcome mental obstacles, achieve your goals, and optimize your golf performance.

Overcoming Distractions

Distractions can be detrimental to your golf game. They can take your focus away from the task at hand and cause you to make costly mistakes. As a golfer, it's important to learn how to overcome distractions and maintain your focus on the course. Here are some tips and strategies to help you do just that.

Develop Laser Focus

One of the best ways to overcome distractions is to develop laser focus. This means training your mind to stay focused on the present moment and the shot at hand. You can do this by practicing mindfulness and meditation. These techniques can help you develop the ability to tune out distractions and stay focused on the task at hand.

Visualization

Visualization is another powerful tool for overcoming distractions. By visualizing your shot before you take it, you can block out distractions and stay focused on your target. Visualization can also help you build confidence and reduce anxiety, which can be major distractions on the course.

Positive Thinking

Positive thinking is another key tool for overcoming distractions. By focusing on positive thoughts and feelings, you can stay motivated and optimistic, even in the face of challenges. This can help you stay focused and perform at your best, even when distractions are present.

Mental Stamina Training

Mental stamina training can help you build the mental toughness you need to overcome distractions. This type of training involves challenging yourself mentally and emotionally, pushing yourself to stay focused and motivated even when things get tough. By building mental stamina, you can stay focused and perform at your best, no matter what distractions may come your way.

Relaxation Techniques

Finally, relaxation techniques can help you overcome distractions by reducing stress and anxiety. By learning to relax your mind and body, you can stay focused and perform at your best even in high-pressure situations. Techniques like deep breathing, progressive muscle relaxation, and guided imagery can all be powerful tools for reducing stress and improving your mental game.

In conclusion, distractions are a part of life, but they don't have to ruin your golf game. By developing laser focus, using visualization and positive thinking, building mental stamina, and practicing relaxation techniques, you can overcome distractions and perform at your best on the course. Remember, the mental game is just as important as the physical game, so take the time to develop a strong and resilient golf mindset.

Staying Focused Through Adversity

Golf is a game that requires a lot of mental focus and concentration. It's not just about hitting the ball, it's about staying focused on your game plan, your swing, and your target. However, golfers often face adversity that can easily break their concentration and focus. This is where mental toughness comes into play.

Adversity can come in many forms, such as weather changes, slow play, noisy crowds, or even personal issues. Whatever the situation, it's essential to stay focused and maintain your mental strength. Here are some tips to help you stay focused through adversity:

Develop Laser Focus

To stay focused, you need to develop laser focus. This means concentrating on your game, ignoring distractions, and staying in the present moment. One way to achieve this is by using visualization.

Golf Visualization Techniques for Improved Focus

Visualization is a powerful tool for improving focus. It involves creating a mental image of your desired outcome, such as hitting the perfect shot. By visualizing success, you can stay focused and motivated, even when facing adversity.

25

The Power of Positive Thinking in Golf

Positive thinking is another essential aspect of staying focused through adversity. By focusing on positive outcomes, you can overcome negative thoughts and stay motivated. One way to achieve this is by using affirmations.

Mental Stamina Training for Golfers

Mental stamina is the ability to stay focused and maintain mental strength over a long period. To develop mental stamina, you need to practice mental exercises that challenge your focus and concentration.

Relaxation Techniques for Better Golf Performance

Relaxation techniques are essential for maintaining focus and concentration. By practicing relaxation techniques, you can reduce stress and anxiety, which can negatively impact your golf performance.

Developing a Strong and Resilient Golf Mindset

To stay focused through adversity, you need to develop a strong and resilient golf mindset. This means staying positive, maintaining mental strength, and overcoming obstacles.

Overcoming Mental Obstacles on the Golf Course

Mental obstacles can come in many forms, such as negative thoughts, self-doubt, or fear. To overcome mental obstacles, you need to develop mental toughness and stay focused on your game plan.

Building Confidence Through Mental Exercises in Golf

Confidence is essential for staying focused and maintaining mental strength. To build confidence, you need to practice mental exercises that challenge your focus and concentration.

Mindfulness and Meditation for Golfers

Mindfulness and meditation are powerful tools for improving focus and concentration. By practicing mindfulness and meditation, you can reduce stress and anxiety, which can negatively impact your golf performance.

Goal Setting and Achievement in Golf Through Mindset Training

Goal setting is an essential aspect of staying focused and motivated. By setting goals and working towards them, you can maintain mental strength and stay focused through adversity.

The Mental Game of Golf: Strategies for Success

The mental game of golf involves staying focused, maintaining mental strength, and overcoming obstacles. By practicing mental exercises and developing a strong golf mindset, you can achieve success on the course.

Chapter 2
Visualization Techniques for Improved Focus

The Science of Visualization

Visualization is a powerful tool that can help golfers improve their performance on the course. It involves creating mental images of the desired outcome, and it has been proven to be an effective technique for improving focus, increasing confidence, and reducing anxiety.

The brain processes visual information faster than any other type of information, making visualization a powerful technique for improving golf performance. By visualizing shots, golfers can program their minds to perform the desired action, creating muscle memory that can improve their swing and overall game.

Visualization is an essential mental skill that helps golfers see themselves making perfect shots and performing at their best. By using visualization techniques, golfers can improve their focus and increase their confidence on the course. This chapter provides several visualization exercises to help golfers improve their visualization skills.

Before delving into the exercises, it is essential to understand what visualization is and how it can be beneficial for golfers. Visualization is the process of creating images in your mind that represent something you want to achieve. In the case of golf, visualization involves picturing yourself hitting the ball perfectly and achieving the desired result. By visualizing success, golfers can build confidence and improve their mental game.

Visualization techniques involve creating a mental image of the desired outcome, whether it's hitting a perfect drive or sinking a putt from a difficult angle. Golfers can use visualization to simulate the experience of playing a round of golf, allowing them to mentally rehearse their shots and develop a better understanding of the course.

One of the most effective visualization techniques for golfers is to create a mental image of their ideal swing. This can be done by closing your eyes and picturing yourself swinging the club with perfect form. Imagine the feeling of the club making contact with the ball and the ball soaring effortlessly through the air. By visualizing this ideal swing, golfers can improve their muscle memory and increase their chances of achieving it on the course.

Another visualization technique that can improve focus is the use of mental imagery. This involves creating a mental movie of yourself playing a round of golf and experiencing success. Start by picturing yourself arriving at the course, getting ready to play, and making your way through each hole. As you play, imagine hitting each shot perfectly and making each putt with ease. Visualize the feeling of success and satisfaction as you complete the round. By doing this exercise regularly, golfers can improve their confidence and focus on achieving success on the course.

One useful visualization technique for golfers is the use of affirmations. Affirmations are positive statements that are repeated to oneself to build confidence and focus. Examples of affirmations for golfers include "I am a confident and successful player" or "I am capable of hitting perfect shots." By repeating these affirmations regularly, golfers can build a positive mindset and improve their focus on the course.

Visualization can also be used to manage nerves and anxiety on the course. By creating a mental image of yourself performing well under pressure, golfers can reduce anxiety and improve their performance. Start by picturing yourself in a high-pressure situation, such as hitting a crucial shot. Imagine yourself remaining calm and focused, hitting the shot perfectly, and achieving success. By visualizing success under pressure, golfers can build confidence and improve their mental game.

Positive thinking as detailed in next chapter is a crucial component of visualization, as it helps golfers to eliminate negative thoughts and focus on the task at hand. By visualizing positive outcomes, golfers can build confidence and reduce anxiety, leading to better performance on the course.

Mental stamina is also an important component of visualization, as it requires focus and concentration. Golfers can use visualization techniques to improve their mental stamina, allowing them to stay focused and relaxed throughout the round.

Relaxation techniques are another important aspect of visualization, as they can help golfers to stay calm and focused under pressure. Techniques such as deep breathing and progressive muscle relaxation can help golfers to stay relaxed and mentally tough, even in the face of difficult shots.

Developing a strong and resilient golf mindset is essential for success on the course, and visualization techniques can help golfers to achieve this. By practicing visualization regularly, golfers can develop the mental toughness needed to overcome obstacles and stay focused on their goals.

Meditation and mindfulness techniques can also be effective tools for improving golf performance. By focusing on the present moment and eliminating distractions, golfers can improve their focus and concentration, leading to better performance on the course.

Meditation and mindfulness techniques can be extremely helpful in improving golf performance by training your mind to focus on the present moment and eliminating distractions. Here is an introduction to techniques you can try:

Breathing exercises: Sit comfortably and focus on your breath, inhaling deeply through your nose and exhaling slowly through your mouth. This will help you to calm your mind and body and get into a more focused state.

Visualization: Visualize yourself hitting a perfect shot or sinking a putt. Try to imagine all the details, including the sights, sounds, and feelings associated with the shot.

Body scanning: Take a few minutes to scan your body from head to toe, noticing any areas of tension or discomfort. Then, consciously relax those areas, letting go of any tension or stress.

Mindful awareness: Practice being fully present and aware of your surroundings. Focus on the feel of the grass under your feet, the sound of the birds in the trees, and the sensation of the sun on your skin. By doing this, you'll be less likely to get caught up in distracting thoughts and emotions.

Letting go of negative thoughts: When negative thoughts or self-doubt arise, acknowledge them, but then let them go. You can do this by simply observing them without judgment or by imagining them floating away on a cloud.

By incorporating these techniques into your routine, you'll be better able to focus on the present moment and eliminate distractions, leading to improved focus and concentration and better performance on the golf course.

Goal setting and achievement detailed further in chapter 10 are also important components of visualization, as they allow golfers to focus on their desired outcomes and work towards achieving them. By setting clear goals and visualizing the steps needed to achieve them, golfers can improve their performance and achieve success on the course.

In conclusion, visualization is an essential mental skill for golfers and is a powerful tool that can help golfers to improve their mental game achieving success on the course. The exercises outlined in this chapter, including mental imagery, ideal swing visualization, affirmations, and pressure management, can help golfers improve their visualization skills and achieve success on the course By practicing visualization techniques regularly and incorporating them into their mental game, golfers can develop the focus, confidence, and mental toughness needed to become champions on the course.

The Benefits of Visualization in Golf

Visualization is an essential tool that can help golfers strengthen their mental game and optimize their performance on the course. Visualization is the process of creating a mental image of a desired outcome or result in the mind's eye. When golfers visualize their shots, they help train their minds to focus on the positive outcome, which can help them achieve their goals.

One of the main benefits of visualization in golf is that it helps golfers develop laser focus. By picturing the shot they want to make, golfers can eliminate distractions and concentrate on the task at hand. This mental clarity can help golfers make better decisions and execute their shots with more precision.

Visualization can also help golfers develop mental stamina. Golf is a mentally challenging game, and the ability to stay focused and composed under pressure is crucial. By visualizing themselves making successful shots, golfers can build their confidence and resilience, which can help them stay mentally strong throughout the game.

Relaxation techniques are also an important part of visualization in golf. By taking deep breaths and picturing themselves in a calm and peaceful environment, golfers can reduce their stress levels and stay relaxed on the course. This can help them maintain their focus and mental clarity, even in high-pressure situations.

Another benefit of visualization in golf is that it helps golfers overcome mental obstacles on the course. Golfers often face challenges such as difficult shots, bad weather, and distractions from other players. By visualizing themselves overcoming these obstacles, golfers can develop the mental toughness needed to succeed in these situations.

Visualization is also a powerful tool for building confidence in golf. By picturing themselves making successful shots, golfers can boost their self-esteem and belief in their abilities. This can help them approach their shots with more confidence and make more aggressive decisions on the course.

In conclusion, visualization is an essential tool for golfers who want to strengthen their mental game and optimize their performance on the course. By using visualization techniques, golfers can develop laser focus, mental stamina, relaxation, resilience, and confidence, all of which are crucial for success in golf.

Techniques for Effective Visualization

Visualization is an incredibly powerful tool that can help golfers improve their performance on the course. By visualizing shots and situations ahead of time, golfers can develop the mental focus and clarity needed to execute shots with precision and consistency. In this subchapter, we will explore some of the most effective visualization techniques for golfers looking to optimize their mental game.

One of the most important aspects of effective visualization is specificity. Golfers should aim to create a vivid mental image of the shot they want to hit, including details such as the trajectory, distance, and ball flight. By visualizing the shot in detail, golfers can develop a clearer sense of what they need to do to execute it successfully.

First, let's detail steps in visualizing effectively.

Visualization is a powerful mental tool that can help golfers improve their performance on the course. Here are some detailed steps on how to visualize effectively for golf:

Find a quiet and comfortable place to sit or lie down where you won't be disturbed. Take a few deep breaths to relax your body and clear your mind.

Visualize the course: Start by picturing the course in your mind's eye. Imagine yourself standing on the first tee, looking down the fairway. Visualize the layout of the course, including the bunkers, hazards, and greens.

Visualize the shot: Next, imagine the shot you want to hit. See yourself standing over the ball, visualizing the flight of the ball as it takes off, travels through the air, and lands on the target. Use as much detail as possible, imagining the sound of the club hitting the ball, the feel of the swing, and the flight of the ball.

Use all your senses: Engage all your senses in the visualization process. See the shot in your mind's eye, hear the sound of the ball striking the clubface, feel the swing and the contact with the ball, and even smell the grass or the scent of the trees.

Add emotions: Add positive emotions to your visualization. Imagine the feeling of satisfaction and joy when you hit the shot perfectly. Visualize yourself smiling and feeling confident and proud of your performance.

Repeat and refine: Repeat the visualization process several times, refining and adjusting it as needed to make it more vivid and detailed. You can also visualize different scenarios, such as difficult shots or challenging conditions, to prepare yourself for any situation on the course.

Visualization can be a powerful tool for golfers to improve their performance and build mental toughness. By following these steps and practicing regularly, you can become a more effective visualizer and perform at your best on the course.

To emphasize, a crucial element of visualization is repetition. Golfers should practice visualizing shots repeatedly, both on and off the course. By doing so, they can develop the mental stamina needed to stay focused and engaged throughout an entire round of golf.

Positive thinking is also a key component of effective visualization. Golfers should aim to focus on the outcome they want to achieve, rather than dwelling on potential failures or mistakes. By maintaining a positive mindset, golfers can build confidence and resilience on the course, which can help them perform at their best even under pressure.

Relaxation techniques can also be helpful for golfers looking to optimize their visualization skills. Techniques such as deep breathing, meditation, and progressive muscle relaxation can help golfers stay calm and focused, even in high-pressure situations.

Ultimately, developing a strong and resilient golf mindset requires consistent practice and dedication. By incorporating visualization techniques into their mental game training, golfers can improve their focus, increase their confidence, and perform at their best on the course. Whether you're a beginner or an experienced golfer, these visualization techniques can help you achieve your goals and reach your full potential on the course.

Visualization for Pre-Shot Routines

If you're looking to improve your golf game, then you must know that it's not just about physical ability, but also about mental strength. One of the most powerful mental tools that golfers can use is visualization. Visualization is the process of creating mental images of a desired outcome. It's a technique that can help you to focus your mind and improve your golf game.

Visualization is especially useful when it comes to pre-shot routines. A pre-shot routine is a set of actions that a golfer takes before hitting a shot. These actions help to prepare the golfer mentally and physically for the shot. Visualization can be used to enhance pre-shot routines by creating mental images of how you want the shot to go. This can help to increase your confidence and focus, which will ultimately lead to better golf shots.

To use visualization for pre-shot routines, start by creating a mental image of the shot you want to hit. Imagine the trajectory of the ball, the distance it will travel, and where it will land. Visualize yourself making a perfect swing and hitting the ball exactly where you want it to go. Try to make the mental image as vivid and detailed as possible.

Once you have a clear mental image of the shot, incorporate it into your pre-shot routine. Take a few deep breaths and focus your mind on the mental image of the shot. Visualize yourself making the perfect swing and hitting the ball exactly where you want it to go. This will help to calm your nerves and increase your confidence.

Visualization is a powerful tool that can help golfers to improve their pre-shot routines and ultimately their golf game. By creating a clear mental image of the shot you want to hit, you can increase your confidence and focus, which will lead to better golf shots. Incorporate visualization into your pre-shot routines and watch your game improve.

Chapter 3

The Power of Positive Thinking in Golf

The Impact of Negative Thinking

Negative thinking is a major obstacle that can hinder golf performance. It is a common tendency for golfers to focus on the negative aspects of their game, such as missed shots, bad swings, and poor scores. However, this type of thinking can lead to a downward spiral of negative emotions, which can ultimately affect the golfer's performance on the course.

Negative thoughts can affect a golfer's mindset and lead to self-doubt and anxiety. When a golfer lets negative thoughts take over, it can be difficult to stay focused and confident. This can result in missed shots and poor performance on the course.

Negative thinking can also have physical effects on the body. When a golfer is stressed or anxious, the body can tense up, making it difficult to swing the club properly. This can lead to further frustration and negative thoughts, creating a vicious cycle that can be challenging to break

Overcoming Negative Self-Talk

Negative self-talk can be a golfer's worst enemy. It can lead to self-doubt, anxiety, and a lack of confidence. Overcoming negative self-talk is essential for achieving success in golf. The first step is to recognize when negative self-talk is occurring. Negative thoughts may include phrases such as "I can't do this" or "I'm not good enough." Once you recognize these negative thoughts, you can begin to challenge them.

One effective way to challenge negative self-talk is to reframe the negative thought into a positive one. For example, if you are thinking, "I can't do this," reframe it to, "I am capable of doing this, and I will try my best." Another technique is to use positive affirmations. Affirmations are positive statements that you repeat to yourself to build confidence. For example, "I am a great golfer" or "I can overcome any obstacle in my game.".

To overcome negative thinking, golfers must learn to be aware of their thoughts and emotions. This involves recognizing negative thoughts as they arise and replacing them with positive ones. This can be done through visualization exercises, positive affirmations, and mindfulness practices.

Visualization techniques can help golfers develop laser focus and improve their overall performance on the course. By visualizing successful shots and positive outcomes, golfers can train their minds to focus on the positive aspects of their game.

Positive thinking is also essential for building mental stamina and resilience on the course. Golfers who have a positive attitude are more likely to stay relaxed and mentally tough, even in high-pressure situations.

Relaxation techniques, such as deep breathing and meditation, can also help golfers stay calm and focused on the course. By learning to control their breathing and relax their muscles, golfers can reduce stress and anxiety, allowing them to perform at their best.

In conclusion, negative thinking can have a significant impact on a golfer's game. By developing a strong and resilient mindset, golfers can overcome mental obstacles and build confidence on the course. Through visualization, positive thinking, and relaxation techniques, golfers can optimize their mental game and achieve success on the course.

The Benefits of Positive Thinking

Positive thinking is a powerful tool that can help golfers improve their mental game and optimize their golf performance. It involves focusing on positive thoughts and feelings, rather than negative ones, and can have a profound impact on golfers' mental and physical well-being.

One of the most significant benefits of positive thinking is that it can help golfers develop laser focus on their game. When golfers have a positive mindset, they are better able to concentrate on their shots and stay in the present moment. This, in turn, can help them make better decisions on the course and improve their overall performance.

Positive thinking can also be a great way to visualize success on the golf course. By visualizing shots that are successful, golfers can develop a mental picture of what they want to achieve and work towards it. Visualization can help golfers stay focused and motivated, even when things aren't going their way on the course.

In addition to improving focus and visualization, positive thinking can also help golfers develop the mental stamina needed to perform at their best. Golf can be a mentally and physically demanding sport, and positive thinking can help golfers stay energized and focused throughout the round.

Relaxation techniques are another important aspect of positive thinking in golf. By learning how to keep calm and relaxed on the course, golfers can avoid getting too worked up or stressed out during play. This can help them stay mentally tough and focused, even in challenging situations.

Finally, positive thinking can help golfers build confidence and overcome mental obstacles on the course. By learning to stay positive and focused, golfers can develop a strong and resilient mindset that will help them overcome any obstacles they may encounter on the course.

In summary, positive thinking is a powerful tool that can help golfers improve their mental game and optimize their golf performance. By focusing on positive thoughts and feelings, golfers can develop laser focus, visualization, mental stamina, relaxation, and mental toughness. This, in turn, can help them build confidence, overcome obstacles, and achieve their goals on the golf course.

Techniques for Developing a Positive Mindset

A positive mindset can be the difference between a good and a great golf round. Developing a positive mindset requires practice, patience, and a willingness to change your thought patterns. Here are some techniques to help you cultivate a positive mindset and optimize your golf performance:

1. Develop Laser Focus: To develop a positive mindset, you need to develop laser focus. Focus on the present moment and the task at hand. Don't let your mind wander to past mistakes or future outcomes. Stay in the moment and focus on what you can control.

2. Visualization: Visualization is a powerful technique for developing a positive mindset. Visualize your shots before you take them. Imagine yourself hitting the perfect shot every time. This technique will help you stay focused and confident on the course.

3. Positive Thinking: Positive thinking is essential to developing a positive mindset. Focus on your strengths rather than your weaknesses. Don't dwell on mistakes, instead, focus on what you can do better next time. Stay optimistic and keep a positive attitude.

4. Mental Stamina: Golf is a mentally challenging sport, and you need to have mental stamina to succeed. To develop mental stamina, you need to challenge yourself mentally. Practice mental exercises that

push you out of your comfort zone. This will help you stay focused and mentally tough on the course.

5. Relaxation Techniques: Relaxation techniques can help you stay calm and focused on the golf course. Practice deep breathing exercises or meditation to help you relax and stay centered. This will help you stay focused and perform your best under pressure.

6. Overcoming Mental Obstacles: Golf can be a challenging sport, and you will face mental obstacles on the course. To overcome mental obstacles, you need to develop a resilient mindset. Focus on the solutions rather than the problems. Stay positive and keep a growth mindset.

7. Mindfulness and Meditation: Mindfulness and meditation can help you develop a strong and resilient golf mindset. Practice mindfulness and meditation to help you stay present and focused on the course. This will help you stay calm and centered under pressure.

8. Goal Setting: Goal setting is a powerful technique for developing a positive mindset. Set realistic goals for yourself and work towards achieving them. Focus on the process rather than the outcome. This will help you stay motivated and focused on your golf performance.

In conclusion, developing a positive mindset takes time and practice. Use these techniques to help you cultivate a positive mindset and optimize your golf performance. Stay focused, stay positive, and stay resilient.

Using Affirmations to Boost Confidence

Building Self-Confidence

Self-confidence is essential for success in golf. A confident golfer is more likely to take risks, make decisions, and perform well under pressure. Building self-confidence takes time and effort, but it is achievable. One effective technique for building self-confidence is to focus on your strengths. Identify what you are good at, and use those strengths to build your confidence. For example, if you are a good putter, focus on making more putts during practice rounds.

As a golfer, your mindset plays an important role in your performance on the course. One of the most powerful tools you can use to strengthen your mental game is affirmations. Affirmations are positive statements that you repeat to yourself to help you shift your mindset and boost your confidence. Here are some tips for using affirmations to improve your golf game:

1. Choose the Right Affirmations

The first step in using affirmations is to choose the right ones. Your affirmations should be positive, specific, and focused on your goals. For example, if you struggle with hitting accurate shots off the tee, your affirmation could be "I am a skilled and accurate driver of the golf ball." This statement is positive, specific, and focused on your goal of hitting accurate shots off the tee.

2. Repeat Them Often

The key to making affirmations work is repetition. You need to repeat your affirmations often, ideally multiple times a day. You can say them out loud, write them down, or even record them and listen to them while you're driving or working out. The more you repeat your affirmations, the more they will sink in and become a part of your mindset.

3. Believe in Them

Another important aspect of using affirmations is to believe in them. If you don't believe that your affirmation is true, it won't have the same impact. So, when you repeat your affirmations, try to really feel and believe them. Visualize yourself hitting accurate shots off the tee, sinking putts, and playing your best golf.

4. Use Them During Practice and Competition

Finally, make sure to use your affirmations during practice and competition. Repeat them before you hit a shot, when you're waiting for your turn, or even during your pre-shot routine. The more you use your affirmations on the course, the more they will become a natural part of your mindset.

Affirmations can be a powerful tool for improving your mental game and boosting your confidence on the course. By choosing the right affirmations, repeating them often, believing in them, and using them during practice and competition, you can develop a stronger and more resilient golf mindset.

Another technique for building self-confidence is to practice positive visualization. Imagine yourself performing well on the golf course and achieving your goals. Practice this visualization daily, and it will help to build confidence and self-belief.

Surround yourself with positive people who believe in you and support your goals. Negative people can bring you down and make it difficult to build self-confidence. Seek out people who encourage you and believe in your ability.

The power of positive thinking in golf cannot be underestimated. A positive attitude can be developed through visualization, positive self-talk, and goal-setting. Overcoming negative self-talk involves challenging negative thoughts and using positive affirmations. Building self-confidence takes time and effort but can be achieved through focusing on strengths, positive visualization, and surrounding yourself with positive people. By implementing these techniques, golfers can stay optimistic, confident, and focused under pressure, leading to improved performance on the golf course.

Chapter4

Mental Stamina Training for Golfers

Understanding Mental Endurance

What is Mental Stamina?

Mental stamina refers to the ability to stay mentally strong and focused, even under challenging circumstances. It is a combination of psychological skills such as concentration, attention, motivation, and emotional control. Mental stamina is crucial for golfers because it helps them to stay focused on the game, maintain their energy and intensity, and overcome obstacles such as distractions, pressure, or fatigue.

There are several factors that contribute to mental stamina in golf. Firstly, golfers need to have a clear and focused mind. They need to stay present in the moment, avoid distractions, and concentrate on the shot at hand. Secondly, golfers need to have a positive and resilient attitude. They need to be able to bounce back from setbacks, stay motivated, and remain confident in their abilities. Lastly, golfers need to have good physical and emotional energy. They need to be able to manage their stress levels, maintain their physical fitness and endurance, and regulate their emotions.

Mental endurance is a crucial part of golf, as it allows you to stay focused and perform at your best even when faced with adversity. It involves the ability to maintain your mental energy and focus for prolonged periods, despite the challenges you may encounter during the game. Developing mental endurance is crucial for golfers who want to strengthen their minds and optimize their performance on the course.

One of the primary ways to develop mental endurance is through regular practice. Just as you would practice your swing or putting, you must practice your mental stamina. This can be done by incorporating mental exercises into your daily routine. These exercises can help you maintain your focus and calm your mind, even in the face of distractions and pressure.

Visualization is another powerful tool that can help you develop mental endurance. By visualizing yourself successfully completing a shot or a round, you can improve your focus and confidence, which can help you perform better on the course. Visualization can also help you stay relaxed and mentally tough, even when things aren't going your way.

Positive thinking is another essential component of mental endurance. By focusing on positive thoughts, you can maintain your mental energy and confidence, even when faced with challenges. Positive thinking can help you stay motivated and focused on your goals, which can ultimately lead to better performance on the course.

Relaxation techniques are also crucial for developing mental endurance. By practicing relaxation techniques such as deep breathing or meditation, you can calm your mind and reduce stress, which can help you stay focused and mentally resilient during a round of golf.

Ultimately, developing a strong and resilient golf mindset requires consistent practice and dedication. By incorporating mental exercises, visualization techniques, positive thinking, and relaxation techniques into your routine, you can improve your mental endurance and optimize your performance on the course. By overcoming mental obstacles and building confidence through mindset training, you can achieve your goals and become a successful golfer.

Techniques for Building Mental Stamina

The game of golf is not just about physical ability, but also mental strength. The ability to remain focused, positive, and mentally tough is what separates great golfers from average ones. Building mental stamina is crucial for any golfer who wants to optimize their performance on the course. Here are some techniques followed by exercises for building mental stamina:

Develop Laser Focus: Golf requires intense concentration, and it's easy to get distracted by external factors. One way to build mental stamina is by training yourself to maintain focus. Start by eliminating distractions during practice sessions and rounds. Focus on one shot at a time and visualize the desired outcome.

Visualization: Visualization is a powerful tool that can help golfers build mental stamina. By visualizing successful shots, golfers can create positive mental images that will help them stay confident and focused on the course. Spend time visualizing the perfect shot and feel the emotions associated with it.

Positive Thinking: The power of positive thinking cannot be overstated when it comes to building mental stamina. Golfers who maintain a positive mindset are more likely to succeed on the course. Focus on the things you can control, such as your thoughts and actions, and let go of negative thoughts that can derail your performance.

Relaxation Techniques: Golfers who are relaxed and composed are more likely to perform well under pressure. Practice relaxation techniques such as deep breathing and progressive muscle relaxation to help reduce stress and anxiety on the course.

Mindfulness and Meditation: Mindfulness and meditation are effective techniques for building mental stamina. By focusing on the present moment, golfers can reduce stress and anxiety, increase focus and awareness, and improve overall mental health.

Goal Setting: Setting goals and working towards them is a great way to build mental stamina. Set achievable goals for each round or practice session and track your progress. Celebrate your successes and learn from your failures.

Mental Stamina Training Exercises

Mental stamina training for golfers focuses on developing the psychological skills and strategies needed to improve concentration, motivation, and resilience. Here are some effective exercises that can help golfers build mental stamina:

Visualization: Visualization is a powerful mental tool that can help golfers improve their focus and confidence. Golfers can practice visualization by picturing themselves hitting perfect shots, visualizing the course, and imagining successful outcomes. By doing so, they can train their mind to stay focused on their goals and boost their motivation.

Mindfulness: Mindfulness is a technique that involves paying attention to the present moment, without judgment or distraction. Golfers can practice mindfulness by focusing on their breathing, body sensations, and thoughts. This can help golfers to stay calm, centered, and focused during the game.

Mental Challenges: Mental challenges such as memory games, puzzles, and brain teasers can help golfers improve their cognitive skills and concentration. Golfers can incorporate mental challenges into their daily routine to train their brain to stay alert and focused.

Goal Setting: Goal setting is a powerful tool that can help golfers stay motivated and focused on their objectives. By setting specific, measurable, and achievable goals, golfers can track their progress and maintain their motivation throughout the game.

Positive Self-Talk: Positive self-talk is a technique that involves using positive affirmations and self-talk to boost confidence and motivation. Golfers can use positive self-talk to stay focused, calm, and positive during the game.

Mental stamina training is essential for golfers who aim to improve their game and overcome challenges such as long tournaments, high-pressure situations, and unexpected setbacks. The exercises mentioned in this chapter can help golfers develop endurance and resilience, improve their concentration, motivation, and focus. By incorporating mental stamina training into their routine, golfers can train their mind to stay focused, calm, and positive during the game.

Building mental stamina takes time and practice, but the benefits are worth it. By using these techniques, golfers can develop a strong and resilient mindset that will help them perform at their best on the course.

Overcoming Fatigue and Burnout

Golf is a game that requires a lot of mental toughness and stamina. Golfers need to maintain their focus and concentration throughout the game, and this can be a challenge, especially when playing long rounds. Fatigue and burnout are common issues that golfers face, and they can negatively affect their performance on the course. However, there are various ways to overcome these challenges and improve your mental game.

One of the best ways to overcome fatigue and burnout is by developing mental stamina. Mental stamina is the ability to maintain focus and concentration for an extended period. This skill can be developed through various mental exercises and techniques such as visualization, mindfulness, and meditation. Visualization is a powerful technique that can help golfers improve their focus and concentration.

By visualizing yourself making successful shots and putts, you can build confidence and stay motivated throughout the game.

Positive thinking is another powerful tool that can help golfers overcome fatigue and burnout. When you have a positive mindset, you are more likely to stay motivated and focused on your goals. This can help you overcome obstacles and challenges on the course and improve your overall performance.

Relaxation techniques can also be helpful in overcoming fatigue and burnout. When you are relaxed, you are more likely to stay calm and focused on your game. Techniques such as deep breathing, progressive muscle relaxation, and yoga can help you relax and stay focused throughout the game.

Developing a strong and resilient golf mindset is essential for overcoming mental obstacles on the course. This involves building confidence, staying motivated, and maintaining a positive attitude. By setting realistic goals and focusing on your strengths, you can develop a strong and resilient mindset that will help you overcome any challenges that come your way.

In conclusion, overcoming fatigue and burnout is essential for improving your mental game and optimizing your golf performance. By developing mental stamina, practicing visualization and positive thinking, and using relaxation techniques, you can improve your focus and concentration, stay motivated, and develop a strong and resilient golf mindset. These skills will help you overcome any obstacles on the course and achieve your goals as a golfer.

Developing Resilience in the Face of Adversity

Golf is a sport that requires a strong mindset in addition to physical prowess. Developing resilience in the face of adversity can help golfers perform better on the course and achieve their goals. Resilience is the ability to bounce back from setbacks and overcome obstacles. Here are some strategies for developing resilience in golf:

1. Focus on the present moment: Golfers who can stay present and focused on their current shot are more likely to perform well. Instead of worrying about past mistakes or future outcomes, aim to be fully present and engaged in the present moment.

2. Visualize success: Visualization is a powerful tool for golfers. Before hitting a shot, take a moment to visualize the ball flying towards the target and landing exactly where you want it to. This can help you stay focused and confident.

3. Practice positive thinking: The power of positive thinking should not be underestimated. Golfers who can maintain a positive mindset, even in the face of adversity, are more likely to succeed. Try to reframe negative thoughts into positive ones, and focus on what you can control rather than what you can't.

4. Build mental stamina: Golf is a mentally demanding sport, and building mental stamina is key to performing well. This can be done through mental exercises such as visualization, meditation, and mindfulness.

5. Relaxation techniques: Golfers who can stay relaxed and calm under pressure are more likely to perform well. Experiment with different relaxation techniques such as deep breathing, progressive muscle relaxation, or visualization.

6. Overcoming mental obstacles: Golfers will inevitably face mental obstacles on the course, such as negative self-talk or fear of failure. Learning how to overcome these obstacles is key to developing resilience and performing well.

7. Goal-setting: Setting specific, achievable goals can help golfers stay motivated and focused. Break down larger goals into smaller, more manageable steps, and celebrate each step along the way.

Developing resilience is an important aspect of any athlete's mental game, including in golf. Here are some tips for developing resilience in the face of adversity on the golf course:

Embrace the challenge: Rather than seeing obstacles and setbacks as negative experiences, try to view them as opportunities for growth and learning. Embracing challenges can help you develop a growth mindset and become more resilient.

Practice self-compassion: Be kind to yourself when things don't go as planned. Instead of beating yourself up or getting frustrated, practice self-compassion and remind yourself that mistakes and failures are a natural part of the learning process.

Stay positive: Focus on the positives, even when things aren't going well. Try to find something positive to take away from every round, whether it's a great shot or a lesson learned.

Cultivate mental toughness: Developing mental toughness can help you stay focused and resilient in the face of adversity. Practice mindfulness, visualization, and positive self-talk to build mental toughness and improve your ability to bounce back from setbacks.

Set realistic goals: Setting achievable goals can help you stay motivated and build confidence, even when things aren't going perfectly. Make sure your goals are challenging but realistic, and celebrate your progress along the way.

Remember, developing resilience takes time and practice. By embracing challenges, practicing self-compassion, staying positive, cultivating mental toughness, and setting realistic goals, you can become a more resilient golfer and perform better in the face of adversity.

By developing resilience in the face of adversity, golfers can strengthen their mental game and optimize their performance on the course. Experiment with different strategies and techniques, and remember that mental toughness is just as important as physical skill in golf.

Chapter 5

Relaxation Techniques for Better Golf Performance

The Connection Between Relaxation and Performance

Golf is a demanding sport that requires a great deal of focus, concentration, and skill. The pressure of performing well, particularly in competitive situations, can create anxiety, tension, and stress, which can negatively impact a golfer's performance. Relaxation techniques are essential tools for golfers to help them maintain their focus and composure. This chapter provides several relaxation exercises that can improve golf performance by reducing stress and anxiety levels.

As golfers, we all know that the game is as much mental as it is physical. It's not just about hitting the ball straight or making the perfect putt. It's about being able to stay focused and calm under pressure, and that's where relaxation comes in.

Relaxation is a key component of mental toughness on the golf course. When we are relaxed, we are more focused and can think more clearly. We are also less likely to get distracted by negative thoughts or emotions, which can affect our performance.

One of the best ways to achieve relaxation on the golf course is through deep breathing exercises. By taking slow, deep breaths, we can slow down our heart rate and calm our minds. This can help us to stay focused and present in the moment, which is essential for optimal performance.

Another effective relaxation technique is visualization. By visualizing our shots before we take them, we can reduce anxiety and increase confidence. This technique is particularly useful for golfers who struggle with anxiety or self-doubt on the course.

Positive thinking is also important for relaxation and performance. By focusing on positive thoughts and affirmations, we can reduce stress and increase self-belief. This can help us to stay motivated and focused, even when things don't go as planned.

Mental stamina training is another key aspect of relaxation and performance. By practicing mental exercises and building mental toughness, we can stay focused and calm under pressure. This can help us to perform at our best, even in challenging situations.

Overall, relaxation is an essential component of mental toughness on the golf course. By practicing relaxation techniques and building mental strength, we can optimize our performance and achieve our goals. So next time you hit the course, take a deep breath, visualize your shots, and stay positive. Your mind and your golf game will thank you for it.

Techniques for Relaxation and Stress Reduction

The game of golf is as much a battle of the mind as it is of physical ability. To be successful on the course, you need to have a strong and resilient golf mindset. This means developing laser focus, visualization skills, positive thinking, mental stamina, relaxation techniques, and mental toughness through mental exercises.

Deep Breathing

One of the most effective techniques for relaxation and stress reduction is deep breathing. Deep breathing is an excellent relaxation technique that can help golfers calm their nerves and reduce anxiety levels. When you feel anxious or stressed, take a few deep breaths and focus on your breath. Inhale deeply through your nose, hold for a few seconds, and then exhale slowly through your mouth. This technique helps to slow down your heart rate and calm your mind.

Progressive Muscle Relaxation

Progressive muscle relaxation is another effective technique for golfers to reduce tension and stress levels. This exercise involves tensing and relaxing specific muscle groups, one at a time, to promote relaxation throughout the body. To perform this exercise, golfers should sit or lie down in a comfortable position and focus on their breathing. They should then tense the muscles in their feet and hold for a few seconds before releasing the tension and relaxing the muscles. They should then move up to their calves, then thighs, and continue to work their way up their body until they have relaxed all of their major muscle groups, including their face and neck.

Guided Imagery

Guided imagery is a relaxation exercise that involves listening to a recording or a live guide who provides verbal instructions to help the golfer visualize a peaceful and calming scene. This technique can be particularly useful for golfers who have difficulty clearing their minds or focusing on their breathing. To perform this exercise, golfers should find a quiet and comfortable place to sit or lie down. They should then listen to a guided imagery recording or have a live guide provide them with verbal instructions. The guide will ask them to imagine a peaceful and calming scene, such as a beach, a forest, or a waterfall, and provide instructions on how to create a vivid mental image of the scene.

Visualization

As discussed earlier, visualization is another powerful technique for improving focus and reducing stress. Before a round of golf, visualize yourself hitting perfect shots and making putts. Imagine yourself succeeding on the course and feeling confident and in control. As a reminder, to perform this exercise, golfers should sit or stand in a comfortable position, close their eyes, and visualize a successful shot. They should imagine themselves standing over the ball, taking their swing, and watching the ball fly through the air and land exactly where they want it to. They should visualize every detail of the shot, including the sound of the club hitting the ball and the feel of the swing.

Mindfulness and Meditation

Mindfulness and meditation are also effective techniques for reducing stress and improving focus on the golf course. By practicing mindfulness, you can learn to stay present in the moment and avoid distractions that can affect your performance.

Here are some detailed steps for a golfer practicing mindfulness and meditation to relax for better golf performance:

Find a quiet and comfortable place to sit or lie down where you won't be disturbed. You can sit cross-legged on a cushion, a chair with your feet flat on the ground, or lie down on your back.

Take a few deep breaths: Start by taking a few deep breaths, inhaling through your nose and exhaling through your mouth. As you exhale, feel your body relaxing and letting go of any tension or stress.

Body scan: Take a few minutes to scan your body from head to toe, noticing any areas of tension or discomfort. Then, consciously relax those areas, letting go of any tension or stress. You can also use this technique to become more aware of your body's sensations and movements during your golf swing.

Focus on the breath: Bring your attention to your breath, noticing the sensation of air moving in and out of your body. You can count your breaths, or simply focus on the sensation of breathing. If your mind wanders, gently bring it back to the breath.

Mindful awareness: Practice being fully present and aware of your surroundings. Notice the sounds around you, the sensations in your body, and the thoughts and emotions that arise. Allow them to come and go without judgment, simply observing them as they arise and pass.

Visualization: Once you have settled into a relaxed state, you can use visualization to prepare yourself for your next round of golf. Visualize yourself hitting perfect shots, staying focused and calm, and enjoying the experience of playing golf.

Gratitude practice: Take a few moments to reflect on what you are grateful for in your life, such as your health, your loved ones, or the opportunity to play golf. Gratitude can help shift your mindset to a more positive and relaxed state.

By incorporating these mindfulness and meditation techniques into your practice routine, you can develop a greater sense of relaxation and focus, leading to improved performance on the golf course.

Developing a Relaxation Routine

Section Summary

One of the key aspects of mental toughness on the golf course is the ability to stay relaxed and focused, even in high-pressure situations. Developing a relaxation routine can help you achieve this and improve your golf performance.

Start by finding a quiet and comfortable place where you can relax without distractions. Sit down or lie down, close your eyes, and take a few deep breaths. Focus on your breath and let go of any tension or stress in your body.

Once you feel relaxed, start visualizing yourself on the golf course. Imagine yourself hitting the ball perfectly, with accuracy and power.

Visualize every detail of your shot, including the trajectory, the spin, and the landing spot.

As you visualize your shots, keep your mind focused on the present moment. Don't let your thoughts wander to past mistakes or future worries. Stay in the moment and enjoy the process of playing golf.

You can also use positive affirmations to help you stay relaxed and focused. Repeat phrases like "I am calm and confident" or "I trust my swing" to yourself as you visualize your shots.

Another effective relaxation technique is progressive muscle relaxation. Start by tensing the muscles in your feet and then relaxing them. Move up your body, tensing and relaxing each muscle group until you reach your head.

Incorporate your relaxation routine into your pre-shot routine on the golf course. Take a few deep breaths, visualize your shot, and repeat your positive affirmations before each shot.

By developing a relaxation routine, you can stay calm, focused, and mentally tough on the golf course. Practice your routine regularly to make it a habit and improve your golf performance.

The Benefits of Deep Breathing

Deep breathing is one of the most effective techniques to help golfers develop a strong and resilient mindset. By incorporating deep breathing exercises into their daily routine, golfers can enhance their mental focus, visualization skills, positive thinking, and overall mental stamina. In this subchapter, we will explore the benefits of deep breathing and how it can help golfers optimize their performance on the course.

Deep breathing is a simple yet powerful technique that involves taking long, slow breaths in through the nose and out through the mouth. When practiced regularly, deep breathing can help golfers manage their stress levels, reduce anxiety, and increase their overall sense of well-being. By focusing on their breath, golfers can become more present and aware of their surroundings, which can help them stay calm and focused during high-pressure situations on the course.

One of the biggest benefits of deep breathing is its ability to enhance visualization skills. By focusing on their breath, golfers can visualize themselves executing the perfect shot, which can help them build confidence and improve their overall performance. Deep breathing can also help golfers stay relaxed and mentally tough during challenging situations on the course, allowing them to maintain their focus and composure even under pressure.

In addition to its mental benefits, deep breathing can also have physical benefits for golfers. By taking deep breaths, golfers can improve their oxygenation levels, which can increase their energy and endurance on the course. Deep breathing can also help golfers recover more quickly between shots, allowing them to maintain their focus and energy throughout the round.

Overall, deep breathing is an essential tool for golfers looking to strengthen their mindset and optimize their performance on the course. By incorporating deep breathing exercises into their daily routine, golfers can develop laser focus, visualization skills, positive thinking, mental stamina, relaxation, and mental toughness. With these skills, golfers can overcome mental obstacles, build confidence, and achieve their goals on the course.

Chapter 6

Developing a Strong and Resilient Golf Mindset

The Importance of Mental Toughness in Golf

Golf is a sport that requires not only physical strength but also mental toughness, a strong and resilient mindset. It is a game of precision, concentration, and strategy. A golfer needs to be able to stay focused, motivated, and confident, even when things are not going well.. The ability to control emotions, focus, and remain calm under pressure is what sets apart the best golfers from the rest. Mental toughness is a crucial factor that impacts your golf performance.

Managing Emotions

Emotions can play a significant role in a golfer's mindset. Strong emotions, such as anger or frustration, can negatively impact a golfer's performance. To develop a strong and resilient mindset, a golfer needs to learn how to manage their emotions.

To manage emotions, a golfer should first identify the emotions they are experiencing. They should then try to understand why they are feeling that way. Once they have identified the emotions and the underlying cause, the golfer can then use techniques such as deep breathing or visualization to calm themselves down.

Managing emotions can be challenging, but it is an essential skill for golfers who want to develop a strong and resilient mindset. By learning how to manage their emotions, golfers can stay focused and motivated, even when facing challenges or setbacks.

Developing a Pre-Shot Routine

A pre-shot routine is a series of actions that a golfer takes before hitting a shot. A pre-shot routine can help a golfer develop a strong and resilient mindset by providing a sense of structure and routine. A pre-shot routine can also help a golfer stay focused and calm under pressure.

To develop a pre-shot routine, a golfer should identify the steps they need to take before hitting a shot. This might include visualizing the shot, taking a deep breath, and checking their alignment. The routine should be practiced until it becomes automatic, so that the golfer can repeat it consistently.

Recapping from earlier in book, why mental toughness is important in golf and how you can develop it.

Developing Laser Focus

Golfers who have mental toughness know how to stay focused on their game plan. They can block out distractions and maintain their concentration, even when the going gets tough. With the help of visualization techniques and mental exercises, you can train your mind to develop laser focus.

Positive Thinking

Positive thinking is another crucial factor that impacts golf performance. Golfers who have a positive outlook are more likely to stay motivated, focused, and resilient. The power of positive thinking can influence your golf game significantly.

Mental Stamina

Golf is a long game that requires mental stamina. The ability to remain mentally alert and sharp throughout the game is essential. Mental stamina training can help you develop the endurance needed to stay focused and perform well throughout the round.

Relaxation Techniques

Relaxation techniques, such as deep breathing and meditation, help golfers stay calm and relaxed on the course. Learning to manage stress and anxiety is critical for maintaining a strong and resilient golf mindset.

Overcoming Mental Obstacles

Golfers who have mental toughness know how to overcome mental obstacles such as fear, self-doubt, and negative thoughts. Developing a strong and resilient golf mindset requires learning to manage and overcome mental barriers.

Building Confidence

Confidence is a crucial factor that impacts golf performance. With the help of mental exercises, visualization techniques, and mindfulness practices, you can build your confidence and overcome mental barriers that hold you back

Goal Setting

Setting goals is essential for golfers who want to master their mental game. By setting specific and measurable goals, you can stay focused and motivated throughout the season. Goal setting and achievement through mindset training can help you improve your golf performance.

Mental toughness is a critical factor that impacts golf performance. By developing laser focus, positive thinking, mental stamina, relaxation techniques, and overcoming mental obstacles, you can build a strong and resilient golf mindset. With the help of mental exercises, visualization techniques, mindfulness practices, and goal setting, you can optimize your golf performance and achieve success on the course.

Techniques for Developing Mental Toughness

Golf is a game of both physical and mental toughness. The ability to keep a clear and focused mind amidst the pressure of competition is a key factor in becoming a successful golfer. Mental toughness is not just about being able to perform under pressure, but it's also about developing a strong and resilient mindset that can help you overcome obstacles and reach your goals. Here are some techniques for developing mental toughness that can help you optimize your golf performance:

Develop Laser Focus: Golf requires intense concentration and focus. To develop laser focus, practice mindfulness and visualization techniques. Focus on one shot at a time and visualize yourself hitting it perfectly.

Visualization: Visualization is a powerful technique that can help you improve your golf game. Before each shot, visualize yourself hitting the ball perfectly. This will help you build confidence and improve your focus.

Positive Thinking: Positive thinking is essential for mental toughness. Focus on your strengths and visualize success. Replace negative self-talk with positive affirmations.

Mental Stamina: Mental stamina is the ability to maintain focus and concentration throughout a round of golf. To develop mental stamina, practice deep breathing exercises and meditation techniques. This will help you stay calm and focused under pressure.

Relaxation Techniques: Relaxation techniques such as progressive muscle relaxation, yoga, and meditation can help you stay calm and relaxed on the golf course. This will help you maintain focus and concentration throughout the round.

Developing a Strong and Resilient Mindset: To develop a strong and resilient mindset, practice mental exercises such as visualization, positive thinking, and goal setting. Focus on your strengths and work on improving your weaknesses.

Overcoming Mental Obstacles: Golf is a mental game and you will face obstacles such as self-doubt, anxiety, and frustration. To overcome these obstacles, practice mindfulness and visualization techniques. Focus on the present moment and visualize success.

Building Confidence: Confidence is essential for mental toughness. To build confidence, practice mental exercises such as visualization, positive thinking, and goal setting. Focus on your strengths and work on improving your weaknesses.

Mindfulness and Meditation: Mindfulness and meditation can help you stay calm and focused on the golf course. Practice deep breathing exercises and meditation techniques to maintain focus and concentration throughout the round.

Goal Setting: Goal setting is essential for mental toughness. Set realistic and achievable goals and visualize yourself achieving them. This will help you stay motivated and focused on your golf game.

In conclusion, developing mental toughness is essential for optimizing your golf performance. Practice these techniques to develop laser focus, visualization, positive thinking, mental stamina, relaxation, a strong and resilient mindset, overcoming mental obstacles, building confidence, mindfulness and meditation, and goal setting for success on the golf course.

Overcoming Fear and Anxiety

Fear and anxiety are two of the most powerful emotions that can plague a golfer's mind. They can create a sense of uncertainty and doubt, leading to poor performance on the course. However, it's important to remember that fear and anxiety are normal emotions that everyone experiences from time to time. The key is to learn how to manage them effectively so that you can maintain a strong and resilient golf mindset.

One effective way to overcome fear and anxiety is to develop a sense of laser focus. This means staying fully present in the moment and not allowing your mind to wander to potential outcomes or past mistakes. You can achieve this by practicing visualization techniques that help you to imagine yourself succeeding on the course. By focusing on positive outcomes, you can cultivate a sense of confidence and optimism that can help to counteract feelings of fear and anxiety.

Another way to overcome fear and anxiety is to practice relaxation techniques. Deep breathing exercises, meditation, and mindfulness practices can all help to calm the mind and reduce feelings of stress and anxiety. By learning how to relax your mind and body, you can create a sense of inner peace and tranquility that can help you to perform at your best on the course.

Positive thinking is another powerful tool for overcoming fear and anxiety. By focusing on positive thoughts and affirmations, you can create a sense of confidence and self-belief that can help you to overcome any obstacles that you may encounter on the course. Positive thinking can also help to shift your focus away from potential negative outcomes and towards the possibilities for success.

Finally, it's important to remember that mental toughness is not something that can be developed overnight. It takes time, practice, and dedication to cultivate a strong and resilient golf mindset. By regularly engaging in mental exercises, visualization techniques, and relaxation practices, you can build the mental stamina and resilience needed to overcome fear and anxiety and achieve success on the course.

Building Confidence Through Mental Training

Confidence is key to peak performance in golf. It is the mental state that allows golfers to trust their abilities, take risks, and perform at their highest level. However, confidence can also be fragile and easily shaken by mistakes or setbacks. This is where mental training comes in.

Mental training is the process of developing mental skills that help golfers perform their best under pressure. It involves a range of techniques, including visualization, positive thinking, mental stamina training, relaxation techniques, and mindfulness. Through mental training, golfers can build their confidence, focus, and resilience, and overcome mental obstacles that might hinder their performance.

One of the most effective ways to build confidence through mental training is through visualization. Visualization is the process of imagining yourself succeeding in a particular situation. By visualizing yourself hitting a perfect shot, you are programming your mind to believe that you can do it. This helps to build confidence and reduces anxiety and self-doubt.

Another important aspect of building confidence is positive thinking. Golfers who have a positive attitude are more likely to perform well under pressure. Positive thinking involves focusing on your strengths and successes, rather than dwelling on your mistakes or weaknesses. By reframing negative thoughts into positive ones, golfers can build their confidence and stay motivated.

Mental stamina training is also crucial for building confidence. Mental stamina involves the ability to stay focused and remain calm under pressure. Golfers who have strong mental stamina are better equipped to handle the ups and downs of a round of golf. Mental stamina can be developed through a range of exercises, such as meditation, breathing techniques, and mental imagery.

Relaxation techniques are also essential for building confidence. Golfers who are relaxed and calm are more likely to perform at their best. Relaxation techniques, such as progressive muscle relaxation, deep breathing, and visualization, can help golfers stay calm and focused on the task at hand.

In conclusion, building confidence through mental training is essential for golfers who want to perform at their best. By developing mental skills such as visualization, positive thinking, mental stamina, and relaxation techniques, golfers can build their confidence, focus, and resilience, and overcome mental obstacles that might hinder their performance on the golf course. With a strong and resilient golf mindset, golfers can achieve their goals and succeed in the game of golf.

Chapter 7

Overcoming Mental Obstacles on the Golf Course

Common Mental Obstacles in Golf

Golf is a game of skill, but it's also a game of the mind. Golf is a game that requires a great deal of mental strength and focus. It is not just about hitting the ball, but also about managing your emotions, staying calm under pressure, and maintaining confidence throughout the game. Mental obstacles, such as fear, anxiety, and self-doubt, can significantly impact a golfer's performance and lead to poor scores. Golfers who want to improve their performance and reach their full potential on the course must learn to overcome common mental obstacles that can hinder their progress. In this subchapter, we'll explore some of the most common mental obstacles in golf and provide tips for overcoming them.

One of the most common mental obstacles in golf is self-doubt. Many golfers struggle with negative self-talk that can damage their confidence and prevent them from playing to their full potential. To overcome self-doubt, golfers must learn to recognize their negative thoughts and replace them with positive affirmations. For example, instead of telling yourself "I'll never make this putt," try saying "I've made this putt before and I can do it again."

Another common mental obstacle in golf is fear of failure. Golfers who are afraid of failing often struggle to take risks and make bold shots on the course. To overcome this fear, golfers must learn to embrace failure as a natural part of the learning process. Instead of focusing on the outcome of each shot, focus on the process and the effort you put into each shot.

Another mental obstacle in golf is distraction. Golfers who struggle with distraction often have trouble maintaining focus and concentration throughout a round. To overcome distraction, golfers should practice mindfulness and meditation techniques that can help them focus their attention and block out distractions.

Finally, golfers may struggle with anxiety or nervousness on the course. To overcome this mental obstacle, golfers should learn relaxation techniques such as deep breathing, visualization, and progressive muscle relaxation. These techniques can help golfers calm their nerves and stay focused on the task at hand.

Golfers who want to optimize their performance on the course must learn to overcome common mental obstacles that can hinder their progress. By recognizing negative thoughts, embracing failure, maintaining focus, and practicing relaxation techniques, golfers can develop a strong and resilient golf mindset that will help them reach their full potential on the course.

Techniques for Overcoming Mental Obstacles

Golf is not just a physical game; it's a game of the mind. The mental toughness and focus required to play golf at a high level are just as important as the physical skill. However, mental obstacles can hinder golfers from playing their best game. The good news is that there are techniques for overcoming these mental obstacles.

Developing Laser Focus

Laser focus is the ability to concentrate on a single task without distraction. One way to develop laser focus is to practice mindfulness. During practice, focus on the present moment and pay attention to your breath. When you're playing a round, focus on the shot at hand and block out any distractions.

Visualization

Visualization is a powerful tool that can help golfers improve their game. Visualize the shot before taking it. Imagine the ball's flight path and where it will land. This technique can help golfers feel more confident and prepared before taking a shot.

Positive Thinking

Positive thinking is essential for golfers. It's easy to become frustrated or negative after a bad shot, but it's important to stay positive. Focus on the good shots and visualize future success. Positive thinking can help golfers stay motivated and optimistic.

Mental Stamina

Mental stamina is the ability to maintain focus and concentration throughout a round of golf. Golfers can improve their mental stamina by staying hydrated and taking breaks when needed. Mental exercises, like visualization and mindfulness, can also help improve mental stamina.

Relaxation Techniques

Relaxation techniques can help golfers stay calm and focused on the course. Deep breathing exercises can help reduce tension and anxiety.

Breathing exercises can help you stay calm and focused during the game. Take deep breaths, inhaling for four seconds, holding for four seconds, and exhaling for four seconds. This type of breathing can help reduce anxiety and stress, allowing you to focus on the shot at hand. Yoga and stretching can also help golfers stay relaxed and limber.

Practice Mindfulness

Mindfulness is the practice of staying present in the moment and focusing on your surroundings. When playing golf, it's easy to get stuck in your head and become distracted by negative thoughts. Practicing mindfulness can help you stay focused on the present moment, allowing you to play each shot with intention and purpose.

Overcoming Mental Obstacles

Mental obstacles, like fear and doubt, can hinder golfers from playing their best game. To overcome these obstacles, golfers should practice self-talk. Tell yourself positive affirmations, like "I can do this" or "I am confident." Visualization can also help golfers overcome mental obstacles by visualizing successful shots.

Building Confidence

Confidence is key to success in golf. Mental exercises, like visualization and positive thinking, can help golfers build confidence. Set achievable goals and celebrate small victories to build confidence and maintain motivation.

Reframe Failure

Golf is a game of ups and downs, and it's essential to reframe failure as an opportunity for growth. Instead of dwelling on a bad shot or missed putt, reframe it as a learning experience and an opportunity to improve. This type of mindset can help you stay motivated and resilient throughout the game.

In conclusion, golfers can strengthen their minds and optimize their golf performance by practicing mental techniques like developing laser focus, visualization, positive thinking, mental stamina training, relaxation techniques, and overcoming mental obstacles. These techniques can help golfers develop a strong and resilient golf mindset, build confidence, and achieve their goals on the course.

Dealing with Pressure and Expectations

Golf is a game of mental toughness. On the course, you face a variety of challenges, including pressure and expectations. Whether you're playing in a tournament or just trying to improve your game, it's important to learn how to deal with these challenges and stay focused on your goals.

One of the most effective ways to deal with pressure and expectations is to develop a strong and resilient golf mindset. This involves developing laser focus, visualization, positive thinking, mental stamina, relaxation techniques, and mental toughness through exercises and visualization techniques.

Visualization is an important tool for golfers looking to improve their focus and mental stamina. By visualizing shots and scenarios, you can prepare your mind for the challenges ahead and stay focused on your goals. Visualization can also help you stay relaxed and mentally tough, even under pressure.

Positive thinking is another important ingredient in a strong golf mindset. By focusing on positive thoughts and outcomes, you can improve your confidence and reduce anxiety. This can help you stay focused and perform at your best, even in challenging situations.

Mental stamina is also critical for golfers looking to stay focused and perform at their best. This involves developing the ability to stay focused and maintain your concentration for extended periods of time. You can improve your mental stamina through exercises that challenge your mind and help you stay focused.

Relaxation techniques are also essential for golfers looking to stay calm and focused on the course. Deep breathing, meditation, and other relaxation techniques can help you reduce anxiety and stay calm under pressure. This can help you stay focused on your goals and perform at your best, even in stressful situations.

Finally, it's important to develop a strong and resilient golf mindset that can overcome mental obstacles and setbacks. This involves developing the ability to stay focused and positive, even when things don't go as planned. By building resilience and mental toughness, you can overcome challenges and achieve your goals on the course.

In conclusion, developing a strong golf mindset is essential for golfers looking to improve their mental toughness and optimize their performance on the course. By developing laser focus, visualization, positive thinking, mental stamina, relaxation techniques, and mental toughness through exercises and visualization techniques, you can stay calm, focused, and mentally tough even under pressure and expectations.

Managing Emotions on the Course

Golf is a mentally challenging sport that requires a strong and resilient mindset. As a golfer, it's essential to manage your emotions on the course to optimize your golf performance. Whether you're playing competitively or for leisure, learning to control your emotions can help you play at your best and avoid costly mistakes.

00000One of the most important things you can do to manage your emotions on the course is to develop laser focus. It's easy to get distracted by external factors such as the weather, other players, or your own negative thoughts. However, by practicing visualization techniques for improved focus, you can learn to tune out distractions and stay focused on your game.

Positive thinking is another powerful tool that can help you manage your emotions on the course. By focusing on positive thoughts and affirmations, you can boost your confidence and stay motivated, even when things aren't going your way. Mental stamina training for golfers is also crucial, as it can help you stay mentally strong and resilient in the face of adversity.

Relaxation techniques are also essential for better golf performance. By learning to relax your body and mind, you can reduce tension and anxiety, which can negatively impact your game. Developing a strong and resilient golf mindset requires mental exercises that help you stay calm and focused, even in high-pressure situations.

Overcoming mental obstacles on the golf course is another critical aspect of managing emotions. Whether it's fear of failure, self-doubt, or negative self-talk, learning to overcome these mental barriers can help you play your best golf. Building confidence through mental exercises in golf is also crucial, as it can help you believe in your abilities and play with more confidence.

Mindfulness and meditation are powerful tools that can help golfers manage their emotions and stay focused on the present moment. By practicing mindfulness and meditation, you can learn to stay calm and focused, even in stressful situations. Goal setting and achievement in golf through mindset training is also essential, as it can help you stay motivated and focused on your long-term goals.

In conclusion, managing emotions on the course is a critical aspect of mastering mental toughness in golf. By developing laser focus, visualization, positive thinking, mental stamina, relaxation techniques, a strong and resilient golf mindset, overcoming mental obstacles, building confidence, practicing mindfulness and meditation, and setting and achieving goals, you can optimize your golf performance and achieve success on the course.

Chapter 8

Building Confidence Through Mental Exercises in Golf

The Relationship Between Confidence and Performance

Confidence is a crucial component of success in golf. The more confident a golfer feels, the more likely they are to perform to the best of their abilities. Confidence is not just a feeling; it is a mental state that can be developed and nurtured over time.

The relationship between confidence and performance is a well-established one. Golfers who lack confidence tend to underperform, while those who are confident tend to excel. This is because confidence influences a golfer's mindset and their ability to focus on the task at hand.

Confidence is built through a combination of experience, practice, and mental conditioning. By practicing and gaining experience, golfers can develop a level of competence that translates into confidence. Mental conditioning, such as positive self-talk and visualization exercises, can also help golfers build confidence.

One of the keys to building confidence is setting realistic goals. When golfers set achievable goals and work towards them, they gain a sense of accomplishment that can boost their confidence. Goal-setting also provides a clear direction for golfers to focus their mental energy and effort.

Goal-setting is an important tool for building confidence. By setting achievable goals, you can create a sense of purpose and direction in your golf game. For example, you might set a goal to improve your putting, or to break a certain score by the end of the season.

Once you've set your goals, break them down into smaller, achievable steps. This can help you stay motivated and focused as you work towards your larger goals. As you achieve each smaller step, you'll build confidence and momentum, which can help you achieve your larger goals.

Another important factor in building confidence is staying present in the moment. Golfers who are able to stay focused on the present shot, rather than worrying about past mistakes or future outcomes, are more likely to perform well. Mindfulness and meditation techniques can help golfers stay present and focused on the task at hand.

Confidence is not a fixed state; it can be influenced by a variety of factors, including external circumstances and internal beliefs. Golfers who are able to cultivate a strong and resilient mindset, one that is able to weather setbacks and failures, are more likely to maintain their confidence over time.

In summary, the relationship between confidence and performance in golf is a powerful one. By developing a strong and resilient mindset, setting achievable goals, and staying present in the moment, golfers can build the confidence they need to perform at their best. The mental game of golf is a crucial component of success on the course, and by focusing on mental conditioning and mindset training, golfers can optimize their performance and achieve their goals.

Techniques for Building Confidence

Confidence is a crucial element in the game of golf. It can be the difference between a successful shot and a disappointing one. Many golfers struggle with confidence on the course, but there are techniques that can be used to build and maintain confidence.

One technique for building confidence is visualization. This involves imagining successful shots and positive outcomes. By visualizing success, golfers can create a mental image that can be used as a reference point during actual play. Visualization can help golfers develop laser focus and improve their ability to concentrate on the task at hand.

Positive thinking is another effective technique for building confidence. Golfers can use positive self-talk to reinforce their belief in their abilities. Affirmations such as "I am a great golfer" or "I can make this shot" can help golfers stay focused and motivated.

Mental stamina training is also important for building confidence. Golfers must be able to maintain their mental focus and energy throughout an entire round of golf. Mental exercises, such as meditation and mindfulness, can help golfers develop the mental stamina needed to succeed on the course.

Relaxation techniques are another effective way to build confidence. Golfers can use techniques such as deep breathing and progressive muscle relaxation to reduce tension and anxiety. By staying relaxed, golfers can maintain their focus and perform at their best.

Finally, goal setting and achievement can also help golfers build confidence. By setting achievable goals and working towards them, golfers can build their confidence and self-esteem. Achieving these goals can provide a sense of accomplishment and reinforce the belief in one's abilities.

In conclusion, building confidence is essential for success in the game of golf. By using techniques such as visualization, positive thinking, mental stamina training, relaxation, and goal setting, golfers can strengthen their minds and optimize their golf performance. With a strong and resilient golf mindset, golfers can overcome mental obstacles and achieve their goals on the course.

Overcoming Self-Doubt

Self-doubt is a common enemy of golfers. It can creep up on you when you least expect it, robbing you of your confidence and sabotaging your performance. But the good news is that self-doubt is a mental obstacle that can be overcome with the right mindset and mental exercises.

One of the most effective ways to overcome self-doubt is to develop a strong and resilient golf mindset. This means training yourself to focus on the present moment, visualize success, and stay positive even in the face of adversity. By doing so, you can learn to trust your abilities and overcome any doubts that may arise.

Visualization is a powerful technique that can help you overcome self-doubt and achieve your goals. By visualizing yourself succeeding on the golf course, you can create a mental image of what success looks like and program your mind to believe that it is possible. Visualization can also help you stay focused and relaxed on the course, which can improve your performance.

Positive thinking is another important tool for overcoming self-doubt. By focusing on your strengths and believing in your abilities, you can build confidence and overcome any negative thoughts that may be holding you back. Positive self-talk and affirmations can also help you stay motivated and focused on your goals.

Mental stamina is essential for golfers who want to overcome self-doubt and perform at their best. By training your mind to stay focused and stay calm under pressure, you can develop the mental toughness needed to overcome any obstacles that may arise on the course.

Relaxation techniques, such as deep breathing and progressive muscle relaxation, can also help you overcome self-doubt and improve your golf performance. By learning to relax your body and quiet your mind, you can reduce stress and anxiety, which can help you stay focused and perform at your best.

In conclusion, self-doubt is a common obstacle that all golfers must face. However, by developing a strong and resilient golf mindset, visualizing success, staying positive, building mental stamina, and using relaxation techniques, you can overcome self-doubt and achieve your goals on the course. With the right mindset and mental exercises, you can become a more confident, focused, and mentally tough golfer.

Developing a Positive Self-Image

One of the most important aspects of mental toughness in golf is developing a positive self-image. A positive self-image is the foundation for mental strength and resilience on the course. When you have a positive self-image, you believe in yourself, your abilities, and your potential.

Developing a positive self-image is not something that happens overnight. It requires consistent effort and practice. Here are some tips to help you develop a positive self-image:

1. Focus on your strengths

Everyone has strengths and weaknesses. Instead of focusing on your weaknesses, focus on your strengths. Identify your strengths, and make a conscious effort to build on them. This will help you feel more confident and positive about your abilities.

2. Visualize success

Visualization is a powerful tool for developing a positive self-image. Visualize yourself succeeding on the golf course. Imagine hitting the perfect shot, sinking the putt, and winning the tournament. Visualization can help you build confidence and belief in yourself.

3. Use positive self-talk

The way you talk to yourself has a big impact on your self-image. Use positive self-talk to build yourself up. Instead of saying "I can't do this," say "I can do this." Instead of focusing on your mistakes, focus on what you did well.

4. Set achievable goals

Setting achievable goals can help you build confidence and belief in yourself. Set goals that are challenging but attainable. When you achieve your goals, you will feel a sense of accomplishment and pride.

5. Surround yourself with positivity

Surround yourself with positive people who believe in you and support you. Avoid negative people who bring you down. The people you surround yourself with can have a big impact on your self-image.

Developing a positive self-image takes time and effort, but it is worth it. When you believe in yourself and your abilities, you will perform better on the golf course. You will be more resilient, mentally tough, and confident. So, make a conscious effort to build a positive self-image, and watch your golf game improve.

Chapter 9

Mindfulness and Meditation for Golfers

The Benefits of Mindfulness and Meditation

Golf is a game of patience, concentration, and mental toughness. It requires golfers to stay focused, calm, and present on the course. However, distractions such as negative thoughts, anxiety, and pressure can affect a golfer's performance. Mindfulness and meditation are two powerful tools that can help golfers develop a strong and resilient mindset enhancing their focus, reducing harmful stress, and improving their overall performance These practices have been used for centuries to improve mental clarity, reduce stress, and promote overall well-being. By incorporating mindfulness and meditation into your daily routine, you can optimize your golf performance by cultivating laser focus, visualization, positive thinking, mental stamina, and relaxation.

One of the biggest benefits of mindfulness and meditation is that they help golfers develop laser focus. When you are fully present in the moment, you can block out distractions and concentrate on the task at hand. This is particularly important on the golf course, where a single distraction can throw off your entire game. By practicing mindfulness and meditation, you can train your mind to stay focused and avoid getting sidetracked by external factors.

Visualization is another key benefit of mindfulness and meditation. By visualizing your shots before you take them, you can improve your accuracy and increase your chances of success. Visualization is a powerful technique that can help you overcome mental obstacles on the golf course and build confidence in your abilities.

Positive thinking is also essential to success in golf and can be enhanced through meditation practice. By maintaining a positive attitude, you can stay motivated and focused, even when things are not going your way. Mindfulness and meditation can help you develop a positive mindset by reducing stress and anxiety and promoting feelings of calm and relaxation.

Mental stamina is another important factor in golf performance enhanced by meditation.. By practicing mindfulness and meditation, you can build the mental endurance you need to stay focused and resilient, even in challenging situations. This can help you stay calm under pressure and maintain your focus throughout the entire round.

Finally, mindfulness and meditation can help golfers relax and stay mentally tough. By learning how to quiet your mind and let go of negative thoughts and emotions, you can reduce stress and anxiety and perform at your best. This can help you overcome mental obstacles on the golf course and achieve your goals.

In conclusion, mindfulness and meditation are powerful tools that can help golfers develop a strong and resilient mindset. By incorporating these practices into your daily routine, you can optimize your golf performance and achieve success on the course. Whether you are looking to improve your focus, visualization, positive thinking, mental stamina, or relaxation, mindfulness and meditation can help you achieve your goals and reach your full potential in golf.

Techniques for Mindfulness and Meditation in Golf

Golf is a game that requires both physical and mental stamina. The mental aspect of the game is often overlooked, but it is equally important as the physical aspect. The ability to stay focused, calm, and relaxed under pressure is what separates great golfers from the rest. Mindfulness and meditation techniques can help you develop the mental toughness needed to excel on the golf course.

Mindfulness is the practice of being present in the moment and paying attention to your thoughts and feelings without judgment. In golf, mindfulness can help you stay focused on each shot and not get distracted by external factors. To practice mindfulness, start by taking a few deep breaths and focusing on your breath. Notice any thoughts or feelings that arise and acknowledge them without judgment. Bring your focus back to you

How to Practice Mindfulness in Golf?

Body Scan: To do a body scan, start by standing still and focusing on your breath. Then, move your attention to your feet and slowly scan your body up to your head, noticing any sensations along the way. This exercise can help you become more aware of your body and calm your mind.

Breath Awareness: To practice breath awareness, focus on your breath as you inhale and exhale. Count your breaths or focus on the sensation of air moving in and out of your nose. This exercise can help you stay calm and focused on the course.

Visualization: Visualization is a technique that involves imagining the perfect shot or visualizing yourself achieving your goals. This exercise can help you build confidence and reduce anxiety on the course. r breath and the present moment.

Meditation is a practice of quieting the mind and focusing on a specific object or thought. In golf, meditation can help you visualize your shots and stay calm under pressure. To meditate, find a quiet place where you won't be disturbed. Sit in a comfortable position and close your eyes. Focus on your breath and imagine yourself hitting perfect shots. Visualize the ball flying straight and true to the target. If your mind wanders, gently bring it back to your breath and visualization.

How to Practice Meditation in Golf?

Breath Meditation: To do breath meditation, sit comfortably and focus on your breath as you inhale and exhale. Count your breaths or focus on the sensation of air moving in and out of your nose. This exercise can help you stay calm and focused on the course.

Loving-Kindness Meditation: Loving-kindness meditation is a technique that involves focusing on sending love and kindness to yourself and others. This exercise can help you reduce negative thoughts and emotions on the course.

Mantra Meditation: Mantra meditation involves repeating a word, phrase or sound to achieve a state of relaxation and calm. This exercise can help you stay focused and calm on the course.

Combining mindfulness and meditation with golf visualization techniques can help you develop laser focus and improve your performance on the course. By practicing positive thinking and relaxation methods, you can become mentally tough and overcome any obstacles that come your way.

To develop a strong and resilient golf mindset, it's essential to keep training your mental stamina. Meditation can help you build mental endurance and stay focused for the entire round. You can also use relaxation techniques like deep breathing or progressive muscle relaxation to calm your nerves and reduce tension during the game.

In summary, mindfulness and meditation techniques can help you develop a strong golf mindset and improve your performance on the course. Mindfulness and meditation are powerful mental skills that can help golfers enhance their focus, reduce stress, and improve their overall performance. By practicing mindfulness exercises and meditation techniques regularly, golfers can develop these skills and become more present, calm and focused on the course.

The Role of Mindfulness in Shot Execution

Golf is not only a physical game but also a mental one. The way you approach each shot can have a significant impact on your performance. That's why golfers who want to strengthen their mental game should consider incorporating mindfulness techniques into shot execution.

Mindfulness is the practice of being present in the moment, without judgment, and with full awareness of your surroundings. When applied to golf, mindfulness can help golfers focus better, stay calm under pressure, and make better decisions on the course.

One way to practice mindfulness in golf is by paying attention to your breath. Before each shot, take a deep breath and focus on the sensation of air entering and leaving your body. This simple act can help you calm your nerves and clear your mind, allowing you to focus on the shot at hand.

Another way to incorporate mindfulness into shot execution is by using visualization techniques. Close your eyes and imagine your ideal shot, from start to finish. Visualize the ball's trajectory, the sound it makes as it hits the ground, and how it feels when it lands in the desired spot. This exercise can help you feel more confident and prepared for each shot.

In addition to breathwork and visualization, golfers can also practice mindfulness by staying present and aware of their surroundings. Take in the sights, sounds, and smells of the course, and be fully present in the moment. This can help you stay focused and avoid distractions that may affect your performance.

Overall, practicing mindfulness in shot execution can help golfers develop laser focus, visualization, positive thinking, mental stamina, relaxation, and mental toughness. By incorporating these techniques into your golf game, you can optimize your performance and achieve your goals on the course.

Developing Mental Clarity and Focus

Golf is a game that requires great mental focus and clarity. Every shot demands concentration, and a wandering mind can result in a less than perfect swing. To optimize golf performance, it is essential to develop a strong, focused mindset. Here are some strategies that can help golfers strengthen their mental clarity and focus: These wil seem familiar from earlier in book but its all connected :

Practice mindfulness: Mindfulness involves being fully present and aware of your surroundings, thoughts, and feelings. When you are practicing your golf swings or preparing for a shot, try to focus your attention on the task at hand and avoid distractions. This can help you stay focused and clear-minded during your game.

Visualize success: Visualizing success can be a powerful tool in developing mental clarity and focus. Before taking a shot, take a moment to visualize the perfect shot in your mind. Imagine the ball flying straight and true to the target. This can help you stay focused on the positive outcome you want to achieve.

Set goals: Setting specific goals can help you stay focused and motivated during your game. Set both short-term and long-term goals, and make sure they are realistic and achievable. When you achieve your goals, you will feel a sense of accomplishment and this can help you maintain your focus.

Develop a pre-shot routine: Developing a pre-shot routine can help you stay focused and clear-headed before taking a shot. Your routine might include taking a deep breath, visualizing the shot, and mentally rehearsing your swing. Having a routine can also help you stay calm and confident during your game.

Practice relaxation techniques: Practicing relaxation techniques, such as deep breathing or progressive muscle relaxation, can help you stay calm and focused during your game. When you are feeling anxious or stressed, take a few deep breaths and focus on relaxing your body.

Stay positive: Golf can be a challenging game, and it's important to stay positive and focused on your goals. Instead of dwelling on your mistakes or bad shots, focus on what you can learn from them and how you can improve. Staying positive can help you stay motivated and focused on achieving your goals.

Remember, developing mental clarity and focus takes practice and patience. With consistent effort and a positive attitude, you can improve your mental game and achieve greater success on the golf course.

Develop Laser Focus

To develop a laser focus, golfers need to learn how to concentrate on the task at hand. One effective technique for developing focus is to visualize the shot before taking it. This visualization technique allows golfers to eliminate distractions and focus entirely on the shot. By visualizing the shot, golfers can create a clear picture of what they want to achieve, and this picture helps them stay focused on the task at hand.

Visualization

Visualization is a powerful tool for improving focus and clarity. By visualizing the perfect shot over and over again, golfers can create a mental map of what they want to achieve. This mental map helps golfers stay focused during the shot and improves their chances of success.

Positive Thinking

Positive thinking is another crucial aspect of developing a strong, focused mindset. Golfers should learn to focus on the positives and eliminate negative self-talk. A positive mindset helps golfers stay motivated and focused, even when things do not go as planned.

Mental Stamina

Mental stamina is the ability to stay focused and motivated for an extended period. To develop mental stamina, golfers need to practice mental exercises that challenge their concentration and focus. These exercises can include visualization techniques, breathing exercises, and mindfulness practices.

Relaxation Techniques

Relaxation techniques can help golfers stay calm and focused, even under pressure. These techniques can include deep breathing exercises, progressive muscle relaxation, and meditation. By practicing relaxation techniques regularly, golfers can develop a more relaxed and resilient mindset.

Overcoming Mental Obstacles

Golfers often face mental obstacles on the course, such as fear, anxiety, and self-doubt. To overcome these obstacles, golfers need to develop a resilient mindset that can withstand the challenges of the game. This mindset includes positive self-talk, a focus on the present moment, and the ability to let go of mistakes and move on.

Goal Setting

Setting goals is an essential aspect of developing a strong, focused mindset. Golfers should set both short-term and long-term goals that are specific, measurable, achievable, relevant, and time-bound. By setting goals, golfers can stay motivated and focused on their progress, which can ultimately lead to improved performance on the course.

In conclusion, developing mental clarity and focus is essential for golfers who want to optimize their performance on the course. By practicing visualization techniques, positive thinking, mental stamina training, relaxation techniques, and goal setting, golfers can develop a strong and resilient mindset that can withstand the challenges of the game. With the right mindset, golfers can improve their focus, stay relaxed under pressure, and ultimately achieve success on the course.

Chapter 10

Goal Setting and Achievement in Golf through Mindset Training

The Importance of Goal Setting in Golf

As a golfer, you know that your success on the course is not just about your physical abilities, but also about your mental game. One of the most important aspects of mental toughness is goal setting. Setting goals can help you focus your efforts, measure your progress, and stay motivated throughout your golf journey.

Setting goals is an essential part of any golfer's journey. It is a powerful tool that helps players stay focused, motivated, and committed to their goals. However, setting goals is not just about writing them down or visualizing them; it requires a strong mindset that is trained to focus on the end result and overcome obstacles along the way. This chapter focuses on goal setting and achievement in golf through mindset training.

Mindset training is a process that involves developing a positive attitude, visualizing success, and believing in oneself. It is a technique used by many successful golfers to overcome negative thoughts and emotions that can affect performance. Mindset training can help golfers stay focused, motivated, and committed to their goals, which can ultimately lead to better performance on the course.

In golf, there are two types of goals you should consider: performance goals and process goals. Performance goals are specific outcomes you want to achieve, such as shooting a certain score or winning a tournament. Process goals, on the other hand, are the steps you need to take to achieve your performance goals, such as improving your swing or putting technique.

Setting performance goals is important because it gives you a clear target to aim for. It helps you focus your training and practice sessions and gives you a specific measure of success. However, it's important to remember that you can't always control the outcome of your performance goals. There are many factors outside of your control, such as weather conditions or the performance of your competitors. This is where process goals come in.

Process goals are the building blocks of your success. They help you focus on the things you can control, such as your technique, mindset, and preparation. By setting process goals, you can break down your larger performance goals into smaller, more manageable steps. This makes it easier to measure your progress and adjust your approach as needed.

The first step in setting goals through mindset training is to define what you want to achieve. This can be anything from winning a tournament, improving your handicap, or simply playing better golf.

Once you have defined your goal, it is important to break it down into smaller, achievable steps. This will help you stay motivated and focused on your progress.

When setting goals in golf, it's important to make them SMART: Specific, Measurable, Achievable, Relevant, and Time-bound. This means that your goals should be clear and specific, have a way to measure your progress, be realistic and achievable, relevant to your overall golf goals, and have a deadline for completion. For example, instead of setting a vague goal like "I want to play better golf," a SMART goal would be "I want to improve my score by five strokes in the next six months." This type of goal is specific, measurable, achievable, relevant, and time-bound, making it easier to stay motivated and track progress.

Goal setting is an important part of building a strong and resilient golf mindset. By setting both performance and process goals, you can stay focused, motivated, and on track towards achieving your full potential on the course.

Techniques for Effective Goal Setting

Goal setting is a crucial aspect of mental game training in golf. It is essential to have clear and measurable goals in order to improve your golf performance. Goal setting not only helps you stay on track and focused, but it also boosts your confidence and motivation. Here are some techniques for effective goal setting that can help you enhance your golf mindset and achieve success on the course.

1. Set specific, measurable, and attainable goals

To set effective goals, you need to be clear about what you want to achieve. Make sure your goals are specific, measurable, and attainable. For example, instead of setting a vague goal like "improve my golf game," set a specific goal like "reduce my handicap by three strokes in the next three months." This goal is measurable and attainable, and you can track your progress along the way.

2. Focus on the process, not just the outcome

While it's important to have a specific goal in mind, it's also essential to focus on the process of achieving that goal. This means breaking down your goal into smaller, more manageable steps and focusing on the actions you need to take to achieve your goal. For example, if your goal is to reduce your handicap by three strokes, focus on the process of improving your swing, practicing regularly, and working on your short game.

3. Use visualization techniques

Visualization is a powerful tool used in mindset training for golfers, and it can help you achieve your goals. Visualize yourself achieving your goal and imagine the feelings of success and accomplishment.. It involves picturing yourself achieving your goal in detail, imagining all the sights, sounds, and emotions associated with success. Visualization can help golfers overcome negative thoughts and emotions, increasing their confidence and focus on the course.

Use visualization techniques before and during your rounds to stay focused and motivated

4. Develop a positive mindset

A positive mindset is essential for goal achievement. Focus on your strengths and successes, and use positive self-talk to boost your confidence and motivation. Replace negative thoughts with positive ones, and believe in your ability to achieve your goals.

Positive self-talk is another important aspect of mindset training. It involves using positive affirmations to overcome negative thoughts and emotions, such as self-doubt or fear. Positive self-talk can help golfers stay motivated, confident, and focused on their goals.

To make positive self-talk more effective, it is important to use present tense affirmations, such as "I am a great golfer" or "I can handle any challenge." This type of self-talk can help golfers overcome negative thoughts and emotions, increasing their confidence and focus on the course

5. Review and adjust your goals regularly

Review your goals regularly and adjust them as needed. If you're not making progress towards your goal, reevaluate your approach and adjust your actions accordingly. Remember, goal setting is an ongoing process, and it's essential to stay flexible and adapt to changing circumstances.

Finally, it is important to celebrate your successes along the way. This can help you stay motivated and focused on your progress, increasing your chances of achieving your goal. Celebrate small successes, such as improving your score by a stroke or hitting a great shot, as well as larger successes, such as winning a tournament

In conclusion, effective goal setting is a crucial aspect of mental game training in golf. By setting specific, measurable, and attainable goals, focusing on the process, using visualization techniques, developing a positive mindset, and reviewing and adjusting your goals regularly, you can enhance your golf mindset and achieve success on the course.

Mindset training involves developing a positive attitude, visualizing success, and believing in oneself. Setting SMART goals, visualizing success, using positive self-talk, and celebrating successes along the way are all important aspects of mindset training that can help golfers stay motivated, focused, and committed to their goals. By using these techniques, golfers can overcome negative thoughts and emotions, increasing their confidence and focus on the course, and ultimately achieving their goals.

Overcoming Obstacles to Goal Achievement

As a golfer, it is essential to have a strong and resilient mindset to achieve optimal golf performance. However, obstacles are inevitable, and it is essential to have the mental capacity to overcome them. Here are some of the most common obstacles that golfers face and how to overcome them.

Lack of Focus

One of the significant obstacles that can hinder your golf performance is a lack of focus. Losing focus can make you lose track of your game plan and make it difficult to achieve your goals. To overcome this obstacle, you need to develop laser focus and visualization techniques. Practice visualizing your shots before you take them, and this will help you stay focused on your game plan.

Negative Thinking

Negative thinking can be toxic to your golf game. It can lead to self-doubt, anxiety, and lack of confidence, leading to poor performance. To overcome negative thinking, you need to practice positive thinking. Replace negative thoughts with positive affirmations, and this will help you build confidence and improve your golf performance.

Lack of Mental Stamina

Golf is a mentally and physically demanding sport, and lack of mental stamina can be an obstacle. To overcome this obstacle, you need to train your mind to stay focused and relaxed even under pressure. Mental exercises, such as meditation and mindfulness, can help you develop mental stamina and keep your mind sharp.

Lack of Relaxation

Being relaxed is essential to optimal golf performance. When you are tense, your body and mind are not in sync, and this can lead to poor performance. To overcome this obstacle, you need to practice relaxation techniques such as deep breathing, progressive muscle relaxation, and visualization. These techniques can help you stay relaxed and focused during your game.

Lack of Confidence

Lack of confidence can be a significant obstacle to goal achievement in golf. To overcome this obstacle, you need to build confidence through mental exercises such as positive self-talk, visualization, and goal setting. Set achievable goals and celebrate your achievements, and this will help you build confidence and achieve your goals.

In conclusion, overcoming obstacles to goal achievement in golf requires a strong and resilient mindset. Develop laser focus, visualization, positive thinking, mental stamina, and relaxation techniques to optimize your golf performance. Build confidence through mental exercises, mindfulness, and meditation, and set achievable goals to achieve success in the mental game of golf.

Celebrating Success and Learning from Failure

As a golfer, it's important to acknowledge and celebrate your successes on the course. Whether it's hitting a long drive, sinking a tough putt, or shooting a personal best score, taking time to recognize and appreciate your accomplishments can help build confidence and motivation for future rounds.

At the same time, it's equally important to learn from your failures. Golf is a game of ups and downs, and no one hits every shot perfectly. Instead of dwelling on mistakes, use them as opportunities to learn and grow. Analyze what went wrong and identify areas for improvement. Then, make a plan to address these weaknesses and practice until they become strengths.

One way to celebrate success and learn from failure is to keep a golf journal. Write down your accomplishments and areas for improvement after each round, along with any mental or emotional factors that may have influenced your performance. This can help you track your progress over time and identify patterns in your game.

Keeping a golf journal can have several benefits for golfers, including:

Improved self-awareness: By keeping track of your golf game in a journal, you can gain a better understanding of your strengths and weaknesses, and identify areas where you need to improve.

Enhanced learning: By reflecting on your golf rounds, you can learn from your experiences and mistakes, and develop strategies to improve your game.

Increased motivation: Keeping a record of your progress can be motivating, as you can see how far you've come and set goals for where you want to go.

Better preparation: By reviewing your notes before a round, you can mentally prepare yourself for the course and anticipate any challenges you may face.

When it comes to what to write in a golf journal, here are some more ideas:

Scores and statistics: Record your scores and any relevant statistics, such as fairways hit, greens in regulation, and putts per round.

Course notes: Write down any notes about the course, such as which holes are challenging, where to aim your shots, and any hazards to avoid.

Swing thoughts: Note any swing thoughts or adjustments you made during your round, and how they affected your shots.

Mental game: Record any mental challenges you faced during your round, such as nerves or distractions, and how you overcame them.

Goals and reflections: Write down your goals for your golf game, and reflect on your progress towards achieving them.

Practice notes: Record any practice sessions, including drills and exercises, and how they impacted your game.

Overall, keeping a golf journal can be a helpful tool for improving your game and staying motivated. By recording your experiences and reflecting on your progress, you can develop strategies to achieve your goals and become a better golfer.

Visualization is another powerful tool for both celebrating success and learning from failure. Before a round, visualize yourself hitting great shots and achieving your goals. Imagine the feeling of sinking a long putt or hitting a perfect approach shot. This positive visualization can help build confidence and set the tone for a successful round.

After a round, use visualization to replay your shots and identify areas for improvement. Imagine yourself hitting the shot again, but this time with better technique or a different approach. This mental practice can help reinforce good habits and build mental toughness for future rounds.

Finally, remember that golf is a game and should be enjoyed. Celebrate your successes, learn from your failures, and always maintain a positive attitude. With a strong and resilient golf mindset, you can achieve your goals and reach new levels of performance on the course.

Chapter 11

The Mental Game of Golf
Strategies for Success

Understanding the Mental Game of Golf

Golf is a sport that requires both physical and mental strength. While most golfers focus on improving their swing or their technique, the mental game of golf is equally important. The way you think and feel on the golf course can have a significant impact on your performance. Therefore, it is crucial to understand the mental game of golf and how to develop a strong and resilient mindset.

Golf is a game that is played on the course, but it is won or lost in the mind. The mental game of golf is just as important as the physical game, and it is often the difference between a good golfer and a great one. Chapter eleven discusses the mental game of golf and strategies for success. This chapter brings together all the mental skills and strategies covered in the book and provides a comprehensive framework for developing a strong and resilient golf mindset.

The first strategy for success in the mental game of golf is to stay focused on the present moment. Golfers must learn to let go of the past and not worry about the future. Instead, they should focus on the shot at hand and execute it to the best of their ability. This requires a great deal of mental discipline, but it is essential for success on the golf course.

The second strategy is to control your thoughts and emotions. Golfers must learn to manage their emotions and not let them get the best of them. They must also learn to control their thoughts and not let negative self-talk or distractions affect their game. This requires a great deal of self-awareness and mindfulness, but it is essential for success on the golf course.

Developing Laser Focus

One of the most critical aspects of the mental game of golf is developing laser focus. Golf requires a high level of concentration, and distractions can be detrimental to your game. To develop laser focus, it is essential to practice mindfulness and meditation. These techniques can help you stay present and focused on each shot, which can lead to better results on the course. Make sure to download a free brainwave MP3 to help improve focus with a link from the author at the end of the book.

Visualization Techniques

Visualization is another powerful mental game technique that can help golfers improve their focus and performance. Visualization involves creating mental images of the shots you want to make. By visualizing your shots, you can train your mind to focus on the target and trust your swing.

Golfers must learn to visualize their shots and see themselves executing them successfully. This helps build confidence and reinforces positive thinking. Visualization also helps golfers stay focused on the present moment and not worry about the outcome.

A follow up to this is to develop a pre-shot routine. Golfers must learn to develop a consistent pre-shot routine that helps them stay focused and relaxed. This routine should include visualization, deep breathing, and positive self-talk. By having a routine, golfers can reduce anxiety and improve their chances of success.

The Power of Positive Thinking

Positive thinking is a crucial aspect of the mental game of golf. Golfers who have a positive mindset are more likely to perform well on the course. Positive thinking involves focusing on your strengths and having confidence in your abilities. By focusing on positive thoughts, you can overcome negative self-talk and perform at your best.

Golfers must learn to maintain a positive attitude and not let setbacks or mistakes affect their game. They must also learn to celebrate their successes and build on them. A positive attitude helps golfers stay motivated and focused on their goals.

Mental Stamina Training

Golf is a mentally challenging sport, and it requires a high level of mental stamina. Mental stamina training involves practicing mental exercises that can help you stay focused and resilient on the course. These exercises can include visualization, mindfulness, and positive thinking.

Golfers must learn to bounce back from setbacks and not let them affect their confidence or motivation. They must also learn to adapt to changing conditions and not get discouraged. Resilience helps golfers stay focused on their goals and overcome challenges.

Relaxation Techniques

Relaxation techniques are essential for better golf performance. Golfers who are relaxed and calm on the course are more likely to perform well. Techniques such as deep breathing and progressive muscle relaxation can help golfers stay relaxed and focused during their rounds.

Overcoming Mental Obstacles

Golfers often face mental obstacles on the course, such as fear, doubt, and anxiety. These obstacles can be challenging to overcome, but with the right mindset, they can be conquered. Mental game strategies such as positive thinking and visualization can help golfers overcome these obstacles and perform at their best.

Golfers must learn to push themselves beyond their comfort zone and not let fear or doubt hold them back. They must also learn to stay focused and composed under pressure. Mental toughness helps golfers perform at their best when it matters most.

Building Confidence

Confidence is a crucial aspect of the mental game of golf. Golfers who have confidence in their abilities are more likely to perform well on the course. Mental exercises such as visualization and positive thinking can help golfers build their confidence and perform at their best.

Goal Setting and Achievement

Goal setting is an essential aspect of the mental game of golf. By setting goals, golfers can focus their attention and energy on achieving their objectives. Mental game training can help golfers set realistic and achievable goals and develop the mindset necessary to achieve them.

In conclusion, the mental game of golf is just as important as the physical game. Understanding the mental game of golf and developing a strong and resilient mindset can help golfers perform at their best on the course. By staying focused on the present moment, controlling their thoughts and emotions, visualizing success, developing a pre-shot routine, staying positive, staying resilient, and practicing mental toughness, golfers can develop a strong and resilient golf mindset that will help them succeed on the course, strengthen their mental game and optimize their golf performance.

Techniques for Developing a Winning Mindset

As a golfer, one of the most important aspects of your game is your mindset. The way you think about the game can have a significant impact on your performance on the course. Developing a winning mindset takes practice, patience, and dedication. In this chapter, we will explore some techniques for developing a winning mindset in golf.

Develop Laser Focus

One of the most critical aspects of a winning mindset is the ability to stay focused. Golf requires a high level of concentration, and distractions can quickly derail your game. To develop laser focus, try practicing mindfulness and meditation. These techniques can help you clear your mind and stay present in the moment.

Visualization

Visualization is a powerful tool for golfers. It involves creating a mental image of the shot you want to make, and then executing it in real life. Visualization can help you build confidence, improve your focus, and reduce anxiety on the course. To improve your visualization skills, try practicing visualization exercises before your rounds.

Positive Thinking

Positive thinking is a critical component of a winning mindset. It can help you stay motivated, overcome obstacles, and maintain a positive outlook on the game. To develop positive thinking, try practicing affirmations, gratitude exercises, and positive self-talk.

Mental Stamina

Golf requires mental stamina, just as much as physical stamina. To develop mental stamina, try practicing mental exercises that challenge your focus and concentration. These exercises can help you stay sharp and focused throughout your rounds.

Relaxation Techniques

Relaxation techniques, such as deep breathing, can help you stay calm and centered on the course. When you feel anxious or stressed, take a few deep breaths to calm your nerves and refocus your mind.

Resilience

Golf can be a challenging game, and setbacks are inevitable. To develop a resilient mindset, try practicing mental exercises that challenge your ability to bounce back from setbacks. These exercises can help you stay motivated and focused, even when things aren't going your way.

Overcoming Mental Obstacles

Mental obstacles, such as fear and self-doubt, can hold you back on the course. To overcome these obstacles, try practicing self-awareness and mindfulness. These techniques can help you identify and overcome negative thought patterns that may be hindering your performance.

Goal Setting

Goal setting is an essential component of a winning mindset. To set effective goals, try using the SMART method (Specific, Measurable, Achievable, Relevant, and Time-bound). This approach can help you set realistic goals that are aligned with your values and priorities.

In conclusion, developing a winning mindset in golf takes practice, patience, and dedication. By incorporating these techniques into your mental game, you can improve your focus, visualization skills, positive thinking, mental stamina, resilience, and goal-setting abilities. With a strong and resilient mindset, you can achieve success on the course and beyond.

The Role of Mental Preparation Before a Round

Mental preparation is an essential aspect of golf that every golfer should take very seriously. Golf is a game that requires a combination of physical and mental abilities, and as such, it is crucial for golfers to strengthen their minds before a round. Mental preparation helps golfers to develop the right mindset, focus, and confidence needed to perform well on the course. In this chapter, we will discuss the role of mental preparation before a round and how it can help golfers to optimize their performance and achieve their goals.

Developing Laser Focus

Laser focus is critical for golfers because it helps them to concentrate on the task at hand and block out any distractions. Mental preparation involves developing the ability to focus on the present moment and avoid getting distracted by anything else. One way to develop laser focus is through visualization techniques. By visualizing themselves executing the perfect shot, golfers can train their minds to focus on the task at hand and block out any distractions.

Positive Thinking

Positive thinking is another crucial aspect of mental preparation before a round. Golfers who have a positive attitude and believe in their abilities are more likely to perform well on the course. Positive thinking helps to build confidence, which is essential for golfers who want to succeed. One way to develop a positive mindset is through self-talk. By telling themselves positive affirmations, golfers can boost their confidence and focus on the positive aspects of their game.

Mental Stamina

Mental stamina is the ability to maintain focus and concentration throughout a round of golf. Mental preparation helps golfers to develop the mental stamina needed to perform well on the course. One way to develop mental stamina is through relaxation techniques. By learning how to relax and stay calm under pressure, golfers can maintain their focus and concentration throughout the round.

Overcoming Mental Obstacles

Mental preparation helps golfers to overcome mental obstacles that can prevent them from performing well on the course. Golfers who have a strong and resilient mindset are better equipped to handle the challenges that come with the game. One way to develop a strong and resilient mindset is through mindfulness and meditation. By practicing mindfulness and meditation, golfers can learn how to control their thoughts and emotions and stay focused on the present moment.

Goal Setting

Finally, mental preparation helps golfers to set and achieve their goals. By setting goals and working towards them, golfers can stay motivated and focused on their game. One way to develop goal-setting skills is through visualization techniques. By visualizing themselves achieving their goals, golfers can stay motivated and focused on their game.

In conclusion, mental preparation is a crucial aspect of golf that every golfer should take seriously. By developing laser focus, positive thinking, mental stamina, resilience, and goal-setting skills, golfers can optimize their performance and achieve their goals on the course. Mental preparation is a continuous process that requires practice and discipline, but with time and effort, golfers can develop a strong and resilient mindset that will help them to perform at their best.

The Importance of Mental Recovery After a Round

Mental recovery after a round of golf is just as important as physical recovery. Golfers often overlook the importance of taking care of their mental health after a round. The mental game of golf is just as important as the physical game. If your mind is not right, it can affect your performance in the next round. Therefore, it's important to take the time to recover mentally after a round.

One way to recover mentally is through visualization. Visualization is a technique where you mentally rehearse a shot or a round. It helps you to focus on the positive aspects of your game and visualize success. Visualization is a powerful tool that can help you to stay mentally sharp and focused.

Another way to recover mentally is through mindfulness and meditation. Both of these practices can help you to relax and clear your mind. Mindfulness is the practice of being present in the moment and aware of your thoughts and feelings. Meditation is the practice of focusing your mind on a particular object or thought. Both of these practices can help you to recover from a round of golf and prepare for the next one.

Positive thinking is also an important aspect of mental recovery. It's easy to get down on yourself after a bad round, but it's important to stay positive. Positive thinking can help you to stay motivated and focused on your goals. It can also help you to overcome mental obstacles on the golf course.

Goal setting is another important aspect of mental recovery. Setting goals can help you to stay focused and motivated. It's important to set realistic goals that are achievable. Goals can help you to stay on track and improve your game.

In conclusion, mental recovery after a round of golf is essential for golfers who want to optimize their performance. Visualization, mindfulness and meditation, positive thinking, and goal setting are all important aspects of mental recovery. By taking care of your mental health, you can strengthen your golf mindset and become a mentally tough golfer.

Conclusion

Recap of Key Concepts

In this book, we have discussed various concepts that are crucial for golfers who want to strengthen their minds and optimize their golf performance with mental game. Let us take a quick recap of some of the key concepts that we have learned in this book.

Develop Laser Focus

Laser focus is essential for golfers to achieve their goals. It helps golfers to stay in the present moment and focus on the task at hand. To develop laser focus, golfers need to learn how to block out distractions and concentrate on their game.

Visualization

Visualization is a powerful technique that can help golfers to improve their focus and performance. By visualizing their shots, golfers can train their minds to create the perfect shot, which can lead to better outcomes on the course.

Positive Thinking

The power of positive thinking cannot be overstated when it comes to golf. Positive thinking can help golfers to stay motivated and confident even when things are not going their way. By focusing on positive thoughts, golfers can overcome mental obstacles and achieve their goals.

Mental Stamina Training

Golf is a mentally demanding sport, and golfers need to have the mental stamina to stay focused and perform at their best. Mental stamina training involves exercises that help golfers to build their mental endurance and stay focused for longer periods.

Relaxation Techniques

Relaxation techniques are crucial for golfers to stay calm and composed on the course. By learning how to relax their bodies and minds, golfers can stay focused and perform at their best.

Developing a Strong and Resilient Golf Mindset

Building a strong and resilient golf mindset is essential for golfers who want to achieve their goals. By learning how to overcome mental obstacles and stay focused, golfers can develop a mindset that is resilient and adaptable to any situation.

Goal Setting and Achievement

Goal setting is crucial for golfers who want to improve their game. By setting specific and measurable goals, golfers can stay motivated and focused on their game. With the right mindset and mental exercises, golfers can achieve their goals and take their game to the next level.

In conclusion, mastering mental toughness is essential for golfers who want to optimize their performance on the course. By developing a strong and resilient golf mindset and using mental exercises and techniques such as visualization, positive thinking, and relaxation, golfers can achieve their goals and reach their full potential.

Call to Action

The game of golf is not just physical, it is highly influenced by the mental state of the player. That is why, as a golfer, it is imperative that you focus on developing a strong and resilient golf mindset. While physical practice is important, it is the mental aspect that can make or break your game.

Developing a laser focus is one of the most important aspects of the golf mindset. It is easy to get distracted by the environment or the other players around you. However, by focusing on your game and blocking out distractions, you can improve your performance significantly. Visualization is another technique that can help you develop laser focus. By picturing yourself hitting the perfect shot, you can train your mind to focus on the task at hand and execute it to perfection.

Positive thinking is also a powerful tool in the golf mindset. It can help you stay motivated and confident even in difficult situations. By cultivating a positive attitude, you can approach each shot with renewed energy and enthusiasm, which can lead to better results.

Mental stamina is another crucial aspect of the golf mindset. Golf is a mentally demanding game that requires you to stay focused and alert for hours on end. By practicing mental exercises and techniques, you can train your brain to stay sharp and focused even under pressure.

Relaxation techniques are also important for golfers. The game can be stressful and anxiety-inducing, which can negatively impact your performance. By learning how to relax and stay calm, you can overcome mental obstacles and perform at your best.

Developing a strong and resilient golf mindset takes time and effort, but it is well worth it in the end. By focusing on mental exercises and techniques, you can improve your focus, visualization, positive thinking, mental stamina, and relaxation. These skills can help you overcome obstacles, build confidence, and achieve your goals on the course. So, if you want to optimize your golf performance, start working on your golf mindset today!

Final Thoughts

Congratulations! You have reached the end of The Golf Mindset: Mastering Mental Toughness on the Course. By now, you should have a better understanding of how your mind can affect your golf performance and how you can use mental strategies to improve your game.

Remember, developing a strong and resilient golf mindset takes time and effort. It requires you to be patient, persistent, and disciplined. You must be willing to put in the work, both on and off the course, to strengthen your mental game.

One of the most important things you can do is to develop laser focus. This means staying in the present moment and not allowing distractions to affect your game. Use visualization techniques to help you stay focused and mentally prepared.

Positive thinking is also key to a strong golf mindset. Believe in yourself and your abilities. Use positive self-talk and affirmations to reinforce your confidence and keep your mindset strong.

Mental stamina is another important factor in golf performance. You must be able to stay mentally sharp throughout a round, even when you are feeling tired or frustrated. Use mental exercises and relaxation techniques to help you maintain your focus and energy.

Overcoming mental obstacles is also crucial to success on the golf course. Whether it is fear, anxiety, or self-doubt, you must learn to identify and address these mental barriers. Use mindfulness and meditation to help you stay calm and centered in the face of adversity.

Finally, goal setting and achievement are essential to a strong golf mindset. Set specific, measurable goals for yourself and work towards them consistently. Celebrate your successes and learn from your mistakes.

In conclusion, developing a strong golf mindset requires discipline, patience, and persistence. Use the mental strategies outlined in this book to improve your focus, visualization, positive thinking, mental stamina, relaxation, and resilience. With a strong and resilient mindset, you can achieve success on the golf course and beyond. Good luck!

Additional Mind Resources

Boost Focus with Brainwave Sounds – Free MP3

Receive a free 15-minute brainwave MP3 that you can listen to on the course or even while working,

Nitrofocus is a special audio that uses brainwave sounds to put you in a state of ultra focus. try the free MP3 and loop it for as long as you'd like. visit, NitrofocusMP3.com

Just listen - and increase your output: More focus, productivity & results with this simple collection of MP3s that you can listen to while relaxing or as you play or work, each helping you increase focus .

Self Hypnosis to Make Your Perfect Golf Swing Every Shot –

Get your unconscious mind fully aligned with your golfing goals

Visit https://iqmindbrainlibrary.com/golfing_selfhypnosismp3s/

If you enjoyed this book, please leave a review on Amazon, Thx